The Paris Commune

The Paris Commune

An ode to emancipation

Resistance Books and the IIRE

The Paris Commune: An ode to emancipation

English edition published May 2021
by Resistance Books and
the International Institute for Research and Education
www.resistancebooks.org – www.iire.org

Edited by Terry Conway, Penelope Duggan and Fred Leplat

Cover design by Adam di Chiara

Cover photo: Group of Communards by the colonne Vendôme after it is demolished.

*The Paris Commune: An ode to emancipatio*n is No. 73 of the IIRE Notebooks for Study and Research

ISBN: 978-0-902869-43-1; EISBN: 978-0-902869-44-8

Acknowledgements

Resistance Books and the International Institute for Research and Education are grateful to all the authors for granting us their permission to republish their works in this book. We are also grateful for the permission of the journals and websites where these works were first published. Resistance Books and the IIRE recognize the work carried out by the Marxist Internet Archive for placing in the public domain so many valuable documents which are a tremendous resource for historians and socialists.

Bibliographical references

Rather than include a great number of footnotes in the different articles, many of them referencing the same works, all bibliographical references are listed at the end of the book. There is also a summary list of the main historical figures mentioned.

ABOUT THE AUTHORS

Daniel Bensaïd (1946-2010) was one of France's most prominent Marxist philosophers and wrote extensively on the Paris Commune and many other subjects. He was a leading member of the Fourth International. His books in English are *Marx for Our Times* (2009), *An Impatient Life* (2013), and *Recorded Fragment: Twelve reflections on the 20th Century* (2020).

Olivier Besancenot is a member of the Nouveau Parti Anticapitaliste in France. His recent books include *Que faire de 1917? Une contre-histoire de la révolution russe* (2017), *Le Véritable coût du capital* (2015), and he is co-author with Michael Löwy of *Affinités révolutionnaires: nos étoiles rouges et noires* (2014).

Sandra Bloodworth is a leading member of Socialist Alternative, Australia. She is the author of *How Workers Took Power: the 1917 Russian Revolution* (2008), *A Crime Beyond Denunciation: A Marxist Analysis of Capitalist Crisis* (2008), and co-author of *Rebel Women in Australian Working Class History* (1998). She is one of the editors of *Marxist Left Review.*

Judy Cox is a primary school teacher in London. She is studying for a PhD on the role of women in radical movements in mid-19th century London. She is the author of *Rebellious Daughters of History* (2021) and of *The Women's Revolution: Russia 1905-1917* (2017).

Penelope Duggan is a member of the Fourth International Executive Bureau in Paris, editor of *International Viewpoint* and Fellow of the IIRE Amsterdam. She has edited *Memoirs of a Critical Communist, Towards a history of the Fourth International* by Livio Maitan (2019) and *Recorded Fragments, Twelve reflections on the 20th century* by Daniel Bensaïd (2020).

Mathilde Larrère is a French historian specialising in revolutionary movements in 19th century France. Her recent books include *Rage against the machisme* (2020); *Il était une fois les révolutions* (2019), and is a co-author of *Des intrus en politique. Femmes et minorités: dominations et résistances* (2017).

V.I. Lenin (Vladimir Ilyich Ulyanov, 1870 – 1924) was a leading Russian revolutionary. He was the first and founding head of government of Soviet Russia from 1917 to 1924 and of the Soviet Union from 1922 to 1924.

Michael Löwy is a French-Brazilian Marxist sociologist and philosopher. He serves as Emeritus Research Director at the National Center for Scientific Research (CNRS) in Paris. His works in English include *Why Ecosocialism: For a Red-Green Future* (2018), *The Theory of Revolution in the Young Marx* (2003), and *Fire Alarm. Reading Walter Benjamin's 'On the Concept of History'* (2005).

Kay Mann is a labour historian and teaches sociology at Miami University in Ohio. Mann is a leading member of the revolutionary organization Solidarity. Kay Mann is the author of *Forging Political Identity: Silk and Metal Workers in Lyon, France, 1900-1935* (2010), and of *Struggles New and Old: Yellow Vests, the French Revolution and 21st Century Anti-Capitalism* (2019).

Eric Toussaint is a historian and political scientist. He is the international spokesperson of the CADTM (Committee for the Abolition of Illegitimate Debt) and sits on the Scientific Council of ATTAC France. He is a member of the Fourth International leadership. His recent books in English include *Greece 2015: There was an alternative* (2010), *The Debt System* (2019), and *Bankocracy* (2015).

CONTENTS

Introduction: The Commune is not dead

PENELOPE DUGGAN

Celebrating the 150th anniversary of the Paris Commune is not, and should not be, a simple exercise in historical memory. In the history of the revolutionary Marxist movement it holds a particularly important place because as Ernest Mandel put it:

> The Paris Commune opened the historical era of proletarian and socialist revolutions. It offers us the first historical example of a true dictatorship of the proletariat. It allowed Marx and Lenin to perfect the Marxist theory of the state.[1]

As Lenin pointed out in *The State and Revolution*:

> The only "correction" Marx thought it necessary to make to the *Communist Manifesto* he made on the basis of the revolutionary experience of the Paris Commune. The last pref-

ace to the new German edition of the Communist Manifesto, signed by both its authors, is dated 24 June 1872. In this preface the authors, Karl Marx and Frederick Engels, say that the programme of the Communist Manifesto "has in some details become out-of-date", and then go on to say: "... One thing especially was proved by the Commune, viz., that 'the working class cannot simply lay hold of the ready-made state machinery and wield it for its own purposes'...." The authors took the words that are in single quotation marks in this passage from Marx's book, *The Civil War in France*.

Karl Marx and Frederick Engels were of course not simply observers from across the Channel. They were leaders of the International Workingmen's Association (First International) whose members in Paris were active and leading members of the Commune. Marx had also sent members of the International from London to be on the ground, notably Elisabeth Dmitrieff, and maintained correspondence (despite interruptions given the circumstances) not only with them but also other leading members of the Commune such as Leo Frankel.

The Commune was thus understood not only in the context of the situation in France since the Revolution of 1789, the previous revolutionary episodes of 1830 and 1848, and the Franco-Prussian war, but also for its meaning internationally. Marx wrote to Frankel:

> I have written several hundred letters on behalf of your cause to every corner of the world in which we have branches. The working class, for the rest, was on the side of the Commune from the beginning. [Marx to Leo Frankel, 13 May 1871.]

Elisabeth Dmitrieff's appeal for the creation of the Women's Union for the Defence of Paris and Aid to the Wounded proclaimed that "all the civilized peoples have their eyes on Paris waiting for our victory so that they can in turn free themselves," going on to cite Russia, Ireland, Poland, Spain, Italy, England and Austria. (We note that anti-colonialism was at this point undeveloped even among internationalists!) Nevertheless, to cite Mandel again:

> The Paris Commune opened a new chapter in the tradition of proletarian internationalism, despite its Jacobin-national origin. It thus provided a first example of a process of permanent revolution. We know that it chose as its flag the red flag, that of the Universal Republic of Labour. We also know the prestigious role played by foreign revolutionaries like Frankel and Dombrowski.

The Paris of the Commune was a city that had suffered a siege, was in a country at war and was fighting to defend itself against both the Prussians and the French government which had tried to take the cannon the Parisians had paid for by popular subscription to defend the city. Nevertheless, at the same time as organizing its military defence, and the basic necessities of life such as collective canteens and medical care, the Commune was a moment where ideas of how to organize life differently emerged. Few of these were able to take substantial or practical form in the short time (seventy-two days) that it existed.

However among the radical ideas put forward, discussed and that began to be put into practice were: suspension of rents; requisition of the workshops abandoned by their capitalist owners for workers' cooperatives; separation of church and state; free access to secular education for girls and boys; equal pay (implemented for schoolteachers – one of the few professions where women and men did the same work); the payment of pensions to widows of national guardsmen whether legally married or not and recognition of their children; direct democracy through the accountability of elected representatives. Measures that are not fully achieved worldwide today...

These ideas emerged not only from the debates within and between the different traditions existing in French socialism (Blanquism, Proudhonism or followers of Marx) but also from the rich and creative discussions in the women's clubs and in particular the work of the Women's Union that ensured women's voices were heard and taken into account in the deliberations of the Commune despite the fact women were not part of the electoral process (women's right to vote was not a widespread demand at the time). However, the debates were far from easy and positions far from unanimous.

Nevertheless, "The Paris Commune brilliantly demonstrated that it is possible to combine the dictatorship of the proletariat and the broadest workers' democracy, with freedom of action assured to all currents of the workers' movement." Mandel continued "The audacity of the workers of Paris was remarkable in that the fundamental problems they posed in March 1871 have not yet been resolved."

This has always been true but after a period of lesser interest the Commune is today becoming again a point of reference not only for the radical, Marxist left but for social movements, in France and worldwide. The French *Nuit Debout* movement (arising from protests against proposed labour laws) in 2016 took up an identification with the Commune, as do sectors of the continuing *gilets jaunes* movement today.

Stathis Kouvelakis notes that "[part of the Kurdish national movement] has drawn inspiration from these ideas to inform the 'democratic confederalism' implemented in the northern Syrian ter-

ritories under its control, often termed the 'Rojava commune'."
("On the Paris Commune: Part 1" published on the Verso blog.)

On the occasion of the 150th anniversary there is a flowering of books, broadcasts and other forms of commemoration. Some, notably in France, are institutionalized and treat the Commune as a single, preserved in aspic, historical event. But others are making the links between the experience of the Commune and today's struggles despite the fact that the break, not just temporally but in terms of political references, is much greater between today and the Commune than it was at the 100th anniversary or in the 1930s when the 1936 commemoration in the year of the election of the Popular Front government attracted more than half a million working men and women.

Note

1. Ernest Mandel: *De la Commune a mai 68 : histoire du mouvement ouvrier international*. Ernest Mandel (1923-1995) was a leading member and theoretician of the Fourth International from the immediate postwar period until his death. He was also a renowned economist. Among his best-known books are *Introduction to Marxist Economic Theory* (1968), and *Late Capitalism* (1975).

2

The Paris Commune of 1871

MICHAEL LÖWY

The tradition of the oppressed

There is a wall at the Père Lachaise cemetery in Paris, known as "Le Mur des Fédérés". It was there that the last fighters of the Paris Commune were shot in May 1871, by Versailles troops. Every year, thousands – and sometimes, as in 1971, tens of thousands – of French people, but also people from all over the world, visit this exalted place of memory of the labour movement.

They come alone or in demonstrations, with red flags or flowers, and sometimes sing an old love song, which became the song of the Communards: *Le Temps des Cerises*. We do not pay homage to a man, a hero or a great thinker, but to a crowd of anonymous people whom we refuse to forget.

As Walter Benjamin said in his theses "On the Concept of History" (1940), the struggle for emancipation is waged not only in the name of the future but also in the name of the defeated generations; the memory of enslaved ancestors and their struggles is one of the great sources of moral and political inspiration for revolutionary thought and action.

The Paris Commune is therefore part of what Benjamin calls "the tradition of the oppressed", that is to say, of those privileged ("messianic") moments in history when the lower classes have succeeded, for a while, in breaking the continuity of history, the continuity of oppression; short – too short – periods of freedom, emancipation and justice which will, each time, serve as benchmarks and examples for new battles. Since 1871 it has continued to nourish the reflection and practice of revolutionaries, starting with Marx himself – as well as Bakunin – and then, in the twentieth century, Trotsky and Lenin.

Marx and the 1871 Commune

Despite their disagreements within the First International, Marxists and libertarians worked together in support of the Paris Commune, that first great attempt at "proletarian power" in modern history. Certainly, the respective analyses of Marx and Bakunin on this revolutionary event were poles apart.

We can summarize the theses of the first in the following terms: "the small group of convinced socialists who participated in the Commune were in a very difficult position.... They had to set up a revolutionary government and army against the government and army of Versailles." Faced with this reading of the civil war in France, which opposes two governments and two armies, the anti–state point of view of the second was quite explicit: "It was a revolution against the State itself, of this supernaturalist abortion of society, a resumption by the people for the people of its own social life."

Attentive and informed readers will have made the correction for themselves: the first opinion is that of ... Bakunin in his essay "The Paris Commune and the Idea of the State". While the second is a quote from ... Marx, in his first draft of "The Civil War in France, 1871". We have purposely muddied the waters, to show that the differences – admittedly very real – between Marx and Bakunin, Marxists and libertarians, are not as simple and obvious as is thought.

Moreover, Marx rejoiced in the fact that, during the events of the Commune, the Proudhonians forgot their master's theses, while certain libertarians observed with pleasure that Marx's writings on the Commune abandoned centralism in favour of federalism.

Marx had proposed, as the central political slogan of the International Working Men's Association – the First International – this formula which he inscribed in the Inaugural Address of the IWA in 1864: "The emancipation of the working classes must be conquered by the working classes themselves". If the Commune of 1871 was so important in his eyes, it is precisely because it was the first revolutionary manifestation of this founding principle of the modern working class and socialist movement.

The Commune, Marx wrote in the Address in the name of the First International in 1871, "The Civil War in France" (and in the preparatory notices), was not the regime of a party or of a group, but "essentially a working class government", a "a government of the people by the people", that is to say, "the taking back by the people and for the people of their own social vocation". For that, it was not enough to "conquer" the existing state apparatus: it was necessary to "break" it and replace it by another form of political power, as the Communards did, from their first decree – the abolition of the standing army and its replacement by the armed people. Here is what Marx wrote in a letter to his friend Kugelman on 17 April 1871, thus during the first weeks of the Commune: "If you look at the last chapter of my Eighteenth Brumaire you will find that I say that the next attempt of the French revolution will be no longer, as before, to transfer the bureaucratic–military machine from one hand to another, but to smash it, and this is essential for every real people's revolution on the Continent. And this is what our heroic Party comrades in Paris are attempting."

What seemed to Marx to be decisive was not only the social legislation of the Commune – certain measures of which, such as the transformation of factories abandoned by their owners into workers' cooperatives, had a socialist dynamic – but above all its political significance as *workers' power*. As he wrote in the Address of 1871, "this new Commune, which breaks the power of the modern state" was the work of "plain working men" who "for the first time dared to infringe upon the governmental privilege of their 'natural superiors'".

The Commune was neither a conspiracy nor a sudden surprise attack, it was "the people acting for themselves and by themselves". The correspondent of the *Daily News* newspaper on 6 May found there was no leader exercising "supreme control", which calls for an ironic comment from Marx: "This shocks the bourgeois who wants political idols and 'great men' immensely".

While activists from the First International played an important role in the events, the Commune cannot be explained by the intervention of a vanguard group. In response to the calumnies of reaction, which presented the uprising as a conspiracy hatched by the IWA, Marx wrote: "The police–tinged bourgeois mind naturally figures to itself the International Working Men's Association as acting in the manner of a secret conspiracy, its central body ordering, from time to time, explosions in different countries. Our Association is, in fact, nothing but the international bond between the most advanced working men in the various countries of the civilized world. Wherever, in whatever shape, and under whatever conditions the class struggle obtains any consistency, it is but natural that members of our Association, should stand in the foreground."

If Marx speaks sometimes of workers and sometimes of "people", it is because he was aware that the Commune was not only the work of the proletarian class in the strict sense, but also of sectors of the impoverished middle classes, intellectuals, women from various social strata, students and soldiers, all united around the red flag and the dream of a social republic. Not to mention the peasants, absent from the movement, but without whose support the uprising in Paris could only fail.

Another aspect of the Commune that Marx insists on is its internationalist character. Certainly, the people of Paris rose up in 1871 against the capitulating bourgeois politicians who reconciled with Bismarck and the Prussian army. But this national leap in no way took a nationalist form; not only because of the role of the militants of the French section of the First International, but also because the Commune appealed to combatants from all nations. The solidarity of the International Workingmen's Association, and the meetings in support of the Commune held in Breslau and other German cities, at the initiative of socialist workers, are the expression of this internationalist significance of the uprising of the Parisian people. As Marx wrote in a resolution adopted by a meeting to celebrate the anniversary of the Commune in March 1872, the Communards were the "heroic vanguard" of the "threatening army of the proletariat of the whole world".

There exists, according to Walter Benjamin in his Theses of 1940, a unique constellation between a present moment in the struggle of the oppressed, and a precise event of the past, a unique image of this past which risks disappearing if it is not recognized. This is what happened during the Russian Revolution of 1905. Only Leon Trotsky saw the constellation between the Commune of 1871 and the struggle of the Russian Soviets in 1905: in his preface, written in December 1905, to the Russian edition of Marx's writings on the Commune, he observes that the example of 1871 shows that "It is possible for the workers to come to power in an economically backward country sooner than in an advanced country." However, once in power, Russian workers will be led, like those in the Commune, to take measures which combine the liquidation of absolutism with the socialist revolution.

In 1905–1906, Trotsky was quite isolated in the defence of the 1871 model for the Russian revolution. Even Lenin, despite his criticisms of the Menshevik tactics of supporting the anti–Tsarist bourgeoisie, refused to regard the Commune as an example for the workers' movement in Russia. In his 1905 work, "Two Tactics of Social Democracy", he criticized the Paris Commune for having confused the aims of the struggle for the republic with those of the struggle for socialism; for this reason, it was a form of government which would not resemble that of the future Russian revolutionary democratic government

Things would turn out quite differently in 1917. From the April Theses, Lenin took the Paris Commune as a model for the Republic of Soviets which he proposed as a goal for the Russian revolutionaries, *precisely because it had effected the dialectical fusion* between the struggle for a democratic republic and the struggle for socialism. This idea would also be broadly developed in *State and Revolution* and all Lenin's other writings during the year 1917. The identification with the Communards was so strong that, according to contemporary accounts, Lenin had proudly celebrated the day when – just a few months after October 1917 – the power of the Soviets had succeeded in holding out one day more than the Commune of 1871.

The October revolution is therefore a striking example of this idea proposed by Walter Benjamin in his Theses: any genuine revolu-

AN ODE TO EMANCIPATION

tion is not only a leap towards the future, but also "a tiger leap into the past", a dialectical leap towards a moment in the past laden with "present time" (*Jetztzeit*).

Like Marx and Engels, Lenin and Trotsky criticized certain political or strategic errors of the Commune: for example, not taking the money from the Bank of France, not attacking Versailles, waiting for the enemy in the barricades of each neighbourhood. Nonetheless, they recognized in this event an unprecedented moment in modern history, the first attempt to "storm the heavens", the first experience of social and political emancipation of the oppressed classes.

The relevance of the Paris Commune in the 21st century

Each generation has its own reading, its own interpretation of the Commune of 1871, according to its historical experience, the needs of its present struggle, the aspirations and utopias which motivate it. What would its relevance be today, from the point of view of the radical left and the social and political movements of the early 21st century, from the Zapatistas of Chiapas to the "movement of movements", the global justice movement?

Of course, the vast majority of militants and activists today know little about the Commune. There are nonetheless some affinities and resonances between the experience of the Parisian spring of 1871 and the struggles of today that deserve to be highlighted:

1. The Commune was a movement of self-emancipation, self-organization and initiative from below. No party tried to take the place of the popular classes; no vanguard wanted to "take power" in place of the workers. The militants of the French section of the First International were among the most active

supporters of the popular uprising, but they never wanted to set themselves up as the self-proclaimed "leadership" of the movement, they never attempted to monopolize power, or marginalize other political currents. The representatives of the Commune were democratically elected in the neighbourhoods and subjected to the permanent control of their popular base.

2. In other words: the Commune of 1871 was a pluralist and unitary movement, in which the partisans of Proudhon or (more rarely) of Marx, libertarians and Jacobins, Blanquists and "social republicans" all participated. Of course, there were debates and differences, sometimes even political clashes in the democratically elected bodies of the Commune. But in practice they acted in common, respected each other, focused their fire on the enemy and not on the comrade in struggle with whom they may have had disagreements. The ideological dogmas of each mattered less than the common objectives: social emancipation, the abolition of class privileges. As Marx acknowledged, the Jacobins forgot their authoritarian centralism, and the Proudhonians their "anti–political" principles.

3. As we saw above, it was an authentically internationalist movement, with the participation of fighters from several countries. The Commune elected a Polish revolutionary (Dombrowicz) to the leadership of its militia; a Hungarian–German worker (Leo Frankel) was commissar of labour. Of course, resistance to the Prussian occupation played a decisive role in triggering the Commune, but the appeal of the French insurgents to the people and to German social democracy, inspired by the utopia of the "United States of Europe"

testifies to this internationalist consciousness.

4. Despite the weight of patriarchy in popular culture, the Commune was distinguished by the active and combative participation of women. The libertarian activist Louise Michel and the Russian revolutionary Elisabeth Dmitrieff are among the best known, but thousands of other women – designated with rage and hatred as *pétroleuses* by the Versailles reactionaries – took part in the fighting of April–May 1871. On 13 April, the citizens' delegates sent to the Executive Committee of the Commune an address which stated the will of many women to participate in the defence of Paris, considering that: "The Commune, representative of the great principle proclaiming the annihilation of all privileges, of all inequalities, at the same time is committed to take into account the just demands of the entire population, without distinction of sex – a distinction created and maintained by the need for antagonism on which the privileges of the dominant classes rests". The appeal was signed by the members of the Central Committee of Women Citizens: Adélaïde Valentin, Noëmie Colleville, Marcand, Sophie Graix, Joséphine Pratt, Céline Delvainquier, Aimée Delvainquier, Elisabeth Dmitrieff.

5. Without having a precise socialist programme, the social measures of the Commune – for example, the handing over to the workers of factories abandoned by their bosses – had a radical anti–capitalist dynamic.

It is evident that the characteristics of the popular uprisings of our time – for example, the Zapatista uprising of 1994, that of the people of Buenos Aires in 2001, that which defeated the anti-Chavez coup attempt in Venezuela in 2002, or that against the villainous President Pinera in Chile in 2019 – to mention just a few recent examples from Latin America, are very different from those of the insurgent Paris of 1871. But many aspects of this first attempt at social emancipation of the oppressed retain an astonishing relevance and should be reflected on by the new generations. Without the memory of the past and its struggles there will be no fight for the utopia of the future.

3

Remembering the Paris Commune

KAY MANN

This spring marks the 140th anniversary of the revolt that led to the establishment of the world's first workers' government, the Paris Commune of 1871. The Commune has always had a special place in the hearts and minds of revolutionaries and can inspire today's activist generation with the potential for "power to the people."

Anniversaries of the Commune, like other anniversaries of notable events in socialist and labour history, have been occasions to celebrate working-class struggles and recall their lessons.

The articles, books, pamphlets and public meetings produced on these anniversaries help preserve the memory of these events. In this way, these historical experiences and their lessons become part of the collective memory of the working class, even part of an oppositional working-class culture.

Marxists as well as various currents within anarchism, syndicalism and libertarian communism have also celebrated the memory of the Commune, and claimed its legacy as their own. Marxists see the Commune as an outstanding example of revolutionary working-class energy, determination and creativity.

The lessons drawn from that experience have been foundational in the elaboration of Marxist theory, and on rare occasions, like the Russian Revolution of 1917, have helped guide revolutionary practice.

Karl Marx and Frederick Engels, who were living in England at the time, immediately recognized the revolt in Paris as an authentic working-class uprising, and the government that the Communards established as the first example of the "dictatorship of the proletariat," by which they meant the establishment of a government that was working class in its composition and the direction of its social policies.

Marx followed the events in Paris that spring of 1871 with a particular intensity. His writings, which took the form of addresses to the leadership of the International Workingmen's Association or First International, of which he was an active leader, are still the most insightful analyses of the Commune, and remain among the most profound interpretations of contemporary political events from the standpoint of historical materialist analysis.

Marx and his followers celebrated the revolutionary audacity of the Communards brave enough to "storm the heavens," but didn't hesitate to criticize their mistakes.

Engels' introduction to the 20th anniversary edition of Marx's writing on the Commune, collected into a volume entitled The Civil War in France, remains one of the clearest – and for those unacquainted with French history, most accessible – Marxist accounts and analyses of the Commune.

The Revolution of 1848

Marx's writings on the Paris Commune can be best understood as an extension of his analysis of the revolution of 1848, and Louis Bonaparte's coup d'état of 2 December 1851 against the Republic that issued from the 1848 uprising.

In March 1848 the Orléanist branch of the French monarchy that had taken over from the Bourbons in a revolutionary uprising in July 1830 was overthrown after several days of street fighting.[1] The French events were in fact part of a wave of revolutionary upheaval that erupted throughout Europe in 1848.

As Louis Philippe left the throne, a broad coalition of political figures representing distinct social classes formed a government. The government (all of whom were men) consisted of representatives of financial capital, petty bourgeois democrats, and two workers' delegates, Louis Blanc, a well known pre-Marxist socialist, and Albert, a skilled worker veteran of underground revolutionary labour organizations.

Unsurprisingly, this diverse group soon began to disagree over the course for the new government. As a concession to the working class in a period of exceptional unemployment, national workshops were created to provide work on public works projects.

In June however, class antagonism in the workshops, streets and government reached fever pitch. The conservative-dominated government provoked a showdown by suddenly shutting down the national workshops and ordering the now unemployed masses of workers out of the city.

A five-day armed battle between workers and the government in June ended with a government victory followed by summary executions and mass deportations of worker militants.

For Marx, the "June Days" represented "the first great struggle of the two classes that split modern society. A new government now shorn of working-class and socialist representation had a decidedly conservative, bourgeois profile. Louis Bonaparte, who claimed to be a nephew of Napoleon Bonaparte, was soon elected president with support of these forces. As his term in office came to a close, he and his supporters organized a coup d'état against the parliamentary republican governmental apparatus on 2 December 1851.

Marx's analysis of the meaning of Bonaparte's coup, which he entitled The Eighteenth Brumaire of Louis Bonaparte (a reference to the date in the revolutionary calendar of Napoleon's 1799 coup against the first Republic), written as a series of articles as the events themselves unfolded, is one of Marx's' most insightful political writings. For the next 18 years, while industrial capitalists made fortunes, French workers and peasants endured a political dictatorship where unions were illegal, radical labour organizations like the First International suppressed, and its leaders imprisoned or exiled.

War and revolution

Perhaps the first feature of the Commune that prefigured future revolutionary upheavals (most graphically the Russian Revolution of 1917) was the role of war in provoking a crisis of the regime and precipitating a revolutionary situation. The state-making ambitions of Bonaparte and Prussian Chancellor Otto von Bismarck collided in the summer of 1870 with France declaring war on Prussia. Marx and the International denounced the war and called on French and German workers to refuse support to their respective governments.

The Franco-Prussian war went badly for France. Bonaparte himself was captured at the battle of Sedan on 1-2 September. As France

AN ODE TO EMANCIPATION

surrendered to Prussia, the empire fell and a broad coalition of "Republicans" (that is, those who favour a parliamentary form of government based on various degrees of popular suffrage), running from conservative to radical, declared a Republic.

A provisional government of national defence was formed – once again, a broad republican coalition united around the perception of common goals. Even the legendary revolutionary August Blanqui offered initial support to this government (which later arrested, tried and jailed him). And once again, divergent interests, strategies and goals rooted in antagonistic material interests drove a wedge through the alliance.

The chief difference was over whether or not to continue what had now become a defensive war against Prussia. Bismarck had continued the siege of Paris as a way to gain leverage for deep concessions in territory and war reparations. Bourgeois public opinion and the bourgeois politicians, around Adolphe Thiers (described by Marx as "a monstrous gnome who had charmed the French bourgeoisie for half a century because he was the consummate intellectual expression of their own class corruption"), who had waited in the wings for Bonaparte's empire to end, sought accommodation with Bismarck, while working-class opinion was sharply in favour of continuing a war of national defence.

As Marx tersely explained, "In this conflict between national duty and class interest, the government of National Defence became a government of national defection." Indeed, when push came to shove, the French bourgeoisie preferred national defeat at the hands of Bismarck's Prussia to the prospect of losing control of French society to its own working class.

For all of their differences, Bismarck and the bourgeois politicians in charge of the new Republic agreed that the Commune had to be crushed. Bismarck agreed to withdraw his troops from Paris and allow the French government in Versailles to do the dirty work of repressing the Commune. This was a significant moment in the history of the bourgeoisie as a class.

The great French Revolution of 1789 had demonstrated the revolutionary energy and vision of an ascending bourgeoisie capable of uniting the popular classes below it, peasants for the most part, as well as urban artisans and labourers, in a successful struggle against the monarchy. That bourgeoisie was able to mobilize vast revolutionary armies eager to defend their revolution and nation from a European-wide coalition of counterrevolutionary forces. But the French bourgeoisie of 1871 could no longer claim to represent anyone but its own narrow interests.

The task of national defence as we will see fell to the working class, and its government, the Commune. As Marx himself put it, the Paris Commune represented "the first revolution in which the working class was openly acknowledged as the only class capable of social initiative. "

The Commune and permanent revolution

This prefigures later developments in anti-colonial struggles such as those in 20th century Russia, China, Vietnam and Cuba, where the bourgeoisie proved itself utterly incapable of defending the most elementary tasks of bourgeois nationalism, leaving the realization of the tasks of the bourgeois revolution to the working class.

The Commune can thus be seen as an early illustration of the revolutionary dynamics outlined by Trotsky in his theory of Permanent Revolution.

Trotsky explained how at a certain historical juncture the bourgeoisie becomes incapable of assuring the historical tasks of bourgeois rule, including national defence. This is exactly what happened in the fall and winter of 1870, as the bourgeoisie lost its appetite for a prolonged struggle with Bismarck, while the working people of Paris felt passionately about national defence and came to understand that only they could assure the defence of the country.

The Commune also illustrates the theory of Permanent Revolution in another way: Trotsky's theory explains that once in power, a working-class government would not stop at "bourgeois democratic" tasks. Having assumed power the Commune as we will see, did not merely mount a military defence of the city; it also took significant political and social measures in a decidedly socialist direction.

As the empire fell and bourgeois politicians scrambled to assume leadership of the new Republic in the fall of 1870, two centres of popular power began to form: the committee of 20 arrondissements organized on the basis of Paris' 20 administrative quarters, and the National Guard. Both were profoundly democratized both in terms of their composition and mode of internal functioning. In the months to come, both became key institutions of the revolutionary state that was the Commune.

In the meantime, tension arose between the national government (which had fled to Bordeaux as the Prussians advanced on Paris) and the working populace in the city. As we have seen, the Thiers government cut a deal with the Prussians behind the backs of the people. On 18 March 1871 government troops sought to remove the cannons (which had been purchased by popular inscription) that had been placed in the high grounds of the city – the working-class neighbourhoods of Montmartre and Belleville.

Crowds, led by women workers in particular, rushed into the streets to block the removal of the cannons. Many troops of the line refused to fire on the people as commanded. Two generals, Lacomte and Clement Thomas were disarmed, arrested, and summarily executed that day. The cannons remained in Paris under the watchful eye of the National Guard. The army and government officials withdrew from Paris and established temporary headquarters in Versailles, 25 miles outside the city.

The National Guard assumed power immediately and organized elections, which were held on 26 March. On 28 March, the Commune is "proclaimed," i.e. becomes the governing body of Paris. The election returns gave a decidedly class character to the new government, described by Marx in the following way: "The majority of its members was naturally working men, or acknowledged representatives of the working class." The Commune "was essentially a working class government, the product of the struggle of the producing classes against the appropriating class. "

Worker insurrections in Lyon, Toulouse, Marseilles, and other French cities established Commune-type revolutionary governments, but all were crushed within days.

Workers' democracy

One of the most remarkable and significant aspects of the Commune was its profoundly democratic character. The Commune's elected officials were subject to immediate recall. No public official would be paid more than the average wages of a skilled worker. The Commune only lasted 72 days. But during that time, its government passed and enacted a series of measures that pointed in a socialist direction.

Although Marx criticized the Commune for having failed to nationalize the bank of France, he saw the Commune as beginning the "expropriation of the expropriators." The social measures of the Commune included:

- The separation of Church and State.[2]
- The abolition of existing rents owed and their suspension for the entire period of the siege.
- The abolition of night work for the hundreds of bakers throughout the city.
- The granting of pensions to the unmarried companions and children of National Guards killed in defence of the Commune.
- Decrees demanding that the city's pawnshops return all workmen's tools and household items valued up to 20 francs, pledged during the siege.
- The postponement of commercial debt obligations, and abolition of interest on the debts.
- The right of workers to establish cooperatives in workshops and factories deserted by their owners. In fact, many cooperatives were actually established.

Women were involved in much of the daily associational life that gave the Commune its revolutionary energy. We have already seen how women were at the forefront of the uprising on 18 March. Marx had these women in mind when he wrote that "the real women of Paris showed again at the surface – heroic, noble, and devoted, like the women of antiquity."

Although women were excluded from formal leadership roles in the Commune, some played leadership roles in many mass based committees that sprang up in the spring of 1871. Elizabeth Dmitrieff, a 20-year-old member of the International who was influenced by Marx, organized the Women's Union for the Defence of Paris and Aid to the Wounded, characterized by one historian as an "extraordinarily cohesive and articulate organization in many arrondissements."

Louise Michel was a leading anarchist activist and feminist who was later deported for her role in the Commune. After the general amnesty in 1880 she returned to France and resumed her work as an anarchist speaker, writer, and organizer.

The Commune was consciously internationalist. Its red flag was meant to signify the International Proletariat. Socialist and anarchist activists from other countries played leadership roles in the Commune. Polish nationalist Jaroslaw Dombrowski, a leading Communard General, was killed on a barricade defending the Commune on 23 May.

The Commune took symbolic measures to display its rejection of France's bellicose imperialism. Painter Gustave Courbet, a member of the Commune, organized the toppling of the Vendôme Column, which had been erected to celebrate the Napoleonic empire.[3]

Repression and massacre

Within days of the founding of the Commune, the army and the provisional government began to attack the Commune's outer defences.

The Commune's leaders spent much of their energy organizing the defence of the city. Here they made what Marx regarded as one of the Commune's great mistakes: they failed to rapidly march on Versailles to engage government troops. Had they done this early, they would have dealt a decisive blow and increased the Commune's chances of survival.

On 21 May, the troops from Versailles broke through city fortifications in a poorly guarded section of the city. This began the *semaine sanglante* or Bloody Week: A week of increasingly less organized, desperate pitched battles throughout the city between the defenders of the Commune – virtually all working people – and government troops and culminating in a final battle in *Père Lachaise* cemetery on 28 May.

Communard prisoners that week were summarily executed. In the weeks that followed, up to 30,000 were shot following summary military "trials."[4] Thousands managed to escape to Switzerland, England, Belgium and the United States. Others were deported to faraway French colonial territories like New Caledonia.

The bourgeois press in other countries offered support for the repression. As the Bloody Week began, the 21 May edition of the Chicago Tribune urged the "mowing down" of rebellious Parisians "without compunction or hesitation."

The ferocious repression of the Commune and the thousands of summary executions that followed sent a clear message of the savagery with which the ruling class is capable when their rule is threatened. It was not until 1880 that the Parliament voted an Amnesty for exiled and imprisoned Communards.

Programmatic shortcomings

One of the central shortcomings of the Commune was the programmatic weaknesses of its leadership. A majority were followers of Pierre August Proudhon, the utopian socialist thinker who advocated the creation of worker-owned cooperatives as a solution to capitalist exploitation. A minority were members of the First International.

The International was split between followers of Marx and followers of the Russian anarchist Mikhail Bakunin. Marx's followers were few, but some like Leo Frankel, a member of the Commune's Commission on Labour, Industry, and Exchange and a Hungarian member of the International, corresponded with Marx and sought his advice.

The predominance of Proudhonian thought among radical French workers in the decades preceding the Commune reflected the structure of French society. The particular course of industrial development in France had produced a working class that was still heavily artisanal. Proletarianization – the process by which small landowners and independent craftsmen lose control and ownership of their property – had proceeded more slowly in France than in England, Belgium, Germany and the United States. This was largely the legacy of the French Revolution of 1789-1799, which had transferred large amounts of land from the nobility to the small and medium peasantry.

This smallholding system retarded large scale capitalist agriculture and the rural exodus to cities and industrial centres that would have provided industrial wage labour for manufacturing, as well as a class of consumers of industrial goods, that is, an industrial proletariat. By 1870, the working class in France still retained a heavily artisanal character; an industrial proletariat working in mechanized medium and large factories was only just emerging at this time.

The social and economic relations surrounding their lives and work seemed to many craftsmen to mesh well with the vision of independent craftsmen and the project of worker cooperatives that Proudhon had promoted. Significantly, the French workers' movement was divided until at least the time of the Commune between "collectivists," those favouring the abolition of private property, and "cooperatives" – those seeing the solution to capitalist exploitation in the establishment of worker owned trade cooperatives that would replace private capitalist ownership.

As industrial capitalist development proceeded, the appeal of cooperativism declined and eventually all but disappeared. But in the early 1870s the predominance of small scale artisanal production created the material conditions for the popularity of cooperative schemes. In fact, the Commune actually established cooperatives in shops and factories that had been abandoned by their owners.

Lessons of the Commune

The revolutionary socialist movement has drawn some its most important theoretical, programmatic and practical lessons from the experience of the Paris Commune. Engels, Lenin and Trotsky all drew on the experience of Commune during various debates with reformist opponents in the Second International, most notably Karl Kautsky of the German Social Democratic Party and George Plekhanov of the Russian socialist movement.

Chief among these lessons and debates has been the question of the state, particularly its class nature and its place in the transformation from capitalism to socialism. Marx and Engels themselves regarded this lesson so highly that they included a reference to it in later editions of the Communist Manifesto, something they didn't otherwise do as the Manifesto had become not only a programmatic, but historical document.

Briefly put, the Commune's lesson regarding the state was that as it takes power, the working class cannot simply take hold of the state machinery of the old regime and wield it for its own purposes. That state must be smashed and a new one built on different foundations. This is exactly what the Commune did when it suppressed the standing (bourgeois) army and government and replaced them with a government and an armed force controlled by the producers themselves, in spite of all the contradiction between these measures and the ideological and programmatic convictions of most Communard leaders.[5] Here Marx and Lenin's observations of the necessity of smashing the old state apparatus and on the profoundly democratic functioning of the Commune merge.

The Commune's practice of instant recall of public officials, and the limitation of their salaries to that of a skilled worker, underscored its democratic and plebian nature. The depth and strength of the Commune's democracy was so much greater than that of bourgeois democracy that it was a state of a fundamentally different nature. In other words, the difference between bourgeois and proletarian democracy is not just of scale, but of kind. As Lenin put it in his comments on the Commune in State and Revolution, "This is exactly a case of 'quantity being transformed into quality': democracy, introduced as fully and consistently as is at all conceivable, is transformed from bourgeois democracy into proletarian democracy; from the state (i.e. a special force for the suppression of a particular class) into something which is no longer, properly speaking, the state."

A prime example of the differences between bourgeois and proletarian states was as Marx immediately observed, the ways that the Commune combined both executive and legislative functions in one single democratically controlled governmental body. The question of the state is one of the key lessons of the experience of the Commune. Every subsequent revolution has had to confront this question. This includes the emerging revolutions in Egypt and Tunisia.

Paris Commune to Russian Revolution

Lenin, as both revolutionary leader and Marxist theoretician, drew heavily on Marx and Engels's analyses of the Commune as the Bolshevik Party navigated the revolutionary situation that arose in Russia in the spring of 1917. In State and Revolution, perhaps one of the most remarkable and insightful of all Marxist writings, Lenin looked to the Commune as he sought to chart a revolutionary course in the period following the February 1917 revolution that had overthrown the Czar.

Indeed, there are interesting parallels between the two revolutions. Although the Kerensky government continued Russia's participation in war and the Thiers government wished to rapidly end it, in both cases the government's course was opposite that favoured by their respective working classes. And in both cases, bourgeois governments were overthrown within months by working-class uprisings leading to proletarian governments.

Early soviet democracy bore similar features to the Commune in its class composition, deeply democratic practices, and socialist social measures. But while the Commune was drowned in blood by the forces of bourgeois reaction, the democratic qualities of the Soviet state soon gave way to Stalinist dictatorship.

Reaction and historical memory

The victors over the Commune were anxious to both limit and control the memory of the Commune and its bloody suppression. Care was taken to remove blood from execution sites, and many bodies were transported outside of the city for burial in mass, unmarked graves.

The Catholic Church hierarchy, a particularly reactionary segment of the French ruling class, invested heavily in promoting their version of the events. They erected the Cathedral of Sacré Coeur on the hilltop of Montmartre, the neighbourhood where the revolt had begun on 18 March. The Sacré Coeur was intended to both commemorate the Catholic upper clergy killed as hostages by the Commune in retaliation for summary executions of communard prisoners, and represent the expiation of the sins of the Communards.

The forces of reaction in France worked hard to portray the Communards as a dangerous, depraved cosmopolitan threat to civilization itself, a group that was perhaps not quite human, an image designed to suggest that its brutal repression was just, even necessary.

The myth of the pétroleuses, wild-eyed Amazon women who supposedly torched large section of the city as the siege was brought to its close (and of which no documented evidence exists), added a misogynist twist to this ruling-class portrayal of the Communards.

Reformist socialist, communist, and labour leaders haven't been too anxious either to preserve or celebrate the memory of the Commune. It has been revolutionaries including anarchists, syndicalists, pre-Stalin communists, Trotskyists and leftwing academic historians who have done the most to preserve the memory of the Commune.

In this way, the Commune bears a telling resemblance to the aftermath of the Haymarket affair, which occurred 125 years ago this May.[6] Although the two events cannot be compared in the scope of the murderous repression – the state of Illinois murdered five prisoners including Louis Lingg who committed suicide the night before the execution, and possibly several more in the police riot that ensued following the bomb explosion at the Haymarket on 4 May 1886 – the intensity of the repression reflected the same fearful, vengeful response to working-class power that drove the repression of the Communards. As was the case following the Commune, the memory of Haymarket in public markers of the event was also minimized and given a particular gloss. Although posthumously pardoned in 1893, the Haymarket martyrs were widely portrayed as dangerous violent threats to civilization itself. The Haymarket martyrs saw themselves following in the footsteps of the Communards, and walked to the gallows singing *La Marseillaise*.[7]

To this day, the most widely circulated image of the affair is the drawing published on the cover of Harper's magazine that portrays a crazed looking orator seemingly directing the throwing of a bomb as injured police grimace in pain.

The immigrant origins of seven of the eight men convicted (all but U.S.-born Albert Parsons were German immigrants) were highlighted in ways designed to underscore their un-Americanness. Significantly, reactionary papers such as the Chicago Tribune accused the Haymarket defendants of wishing to replicate the Paris Commune on American soil. In much the same way, U.S. radicals following the Russian Revolution of 1917 were referred to as Bolsheviks. Once again, the immigrant origins of many labour radicals of the time were highlighted.

While France is full of streets named after Adolph Thiers, no official plaques or monuments were erected in memory of the communard victims of bloody repression and retribution. Likewise, there is no official marker commemorating the Haymarket martyrs. A statue in memory of police who died was placed on the site in 1889, but removed after Weathermen (the underground SDS faction) blew it up in 1969 and again in 1970. In 2004 a sculpture and plaque were finally placed at the site, but fall short of properly commemorating the Haymarket martyrs and the labour struggles that formed the backdrop of the affair.

The admirers of the Commune and the Haymarket martyrs have preserved their memories in a positive way. The monument over the graves of the Haymarket martyrs in Waldheim Cemetery outside Chicago has been a shrine to their memory.

In Paris, a procession to the wall of the fédérés, in Père Lachaise Cemetery where the final Communard combatants were lined up and shot on 28 May 1871, and where many leaders of the international labour, socialist and communist movement are buried, has been held nearly every year since 1880. Most years, the numbers of those who march are rather modest. But occasionally, the procession becomes a mass political demonstration.

In 1936 for example, 600,000 people took part in the procession headed by the leaders of the Popular Front coalition – the Communist, Socialist and Radical parties that had come to power in the elections held several weeks earlier. Within weeks, a general strike involving mass factory occupations erupted, a fitting tribute to the Commune on its 65th anniversary.

On this 140th anniversary, we look back to Marx's concluding words in his address to the general council of the first international: "Workers' Paris, with its Commune, will be forever celebrated as the glorious harbinger of a new society. Its martyrs are enshrined in the great heart of the working class." We recall the lessons for revolutionary theory and practice in our own times that is the great legacy of the Commune. At the same time we also remember Marx's observation in The Eighteenth Brumaire that the social revolution "cannot draw its poetry from the past, but only from the future."

Notes

1. The Bourbon dynasty was restored in 1814 following the defeat of Napoleon's empire. The restoration did not however, lead to the restoration of the remnants of Frances' feudal system that had been overthrown in the revolution of 1789.

2. The separation of church and state, an elementary task of the bourgeois revolution had haunted France since the revolution. The Commune severed those ties during its brief life. It was not until 1906 however, that the issue was definitively settled in favour of the separation.

3. Courbet was later forced to personally pay for the repair and restoration of the column. Interestingly, Marx had used the toppling of the Vendôme column as a metaphor for the empire two decades earlier in his *The Eighteenth Brumaire of Louis Bonaparte.*

4. Most historians and other commentators on the repression of the Commune have estimated that 17,000-30,000 insurgents were killed during the Bloody Week and following the summary court martials that took place afterwards. Cambridge historian Robert Tombs has recently challenged that figure, claiming that the actual number killed was probably between 6,000-7,500. Tombs' article and two scholarly responses can be found at the on-line site, H-France, http://www.h-france.net/Salon/h-francesalon.html.

5. As he pointed out to an associate in a letter written during the Commune, Marx had actually anticipated the revolutionary necessity of the smashing of the bourgeois state 20 years earlier in his work *The Eighteenth Brumaire of Louis Bonaparte.* See

"Letter to Dr. Kugelmann, 12 April 1871 in *The Civil War in France*.

6. For more on the memory of the Haymarket Affair see the "Epilogue" in James Green's sympathetic account of the affair, *Death in the Haymarket*, Anchor Books, 2006. The Marseillaise became a revolutionary anthem during the French revolution and remained part of the French revolutionary left until 1888 (a year after the hangings) when the words of the Internationale, written by a Comunard, Eugene Pottiers, during the Bloody Week, were put to music. At that time, the French revolutionary left abandoned the Marseillaise, now the official hymn of the Republic (and its empire), in favour of the internationalist Internationale. Outside of France, *La Marseillaise* continued as a revolutionary anthem.

4

In Memory of the Commune

V.I. LENIN

Forty years have passed since the proclamation of the Paris Commune. In accordance with tradition, the French workers paid homage to the memory of the men and women of the revolution of 18 March 1871, by meetings and demonstrations. At the end of May they will again place wreaths on the graves of the Communards who were shot, the victims of the terrible Bloody Week, and over their graves they will once more vow to fight untiringly until their ideas have triumphed and the cause they bequeathed has been fully achieved.

Why does the proletariat, not only in France but through out the entire world, honour the men and women of the Paris Commune as their predecessors? And what is the heritage of the Commune?

The Commune sprang up spontaneously. No one consciously prepared it in an organized way. The unsuccessful war with Germany, the privations suffered during the siege, the unemployment among the proletariat and the ruin among the lower middle classes; the indignation of the masses against the upper classes and against authorities who had displayed utter incompetence, the vague unrest among the working class, which was discontented with its lot and was striving for a different social system; the reactionary composition of the National Assembly, which roused apprehensions as to the fate of the republic - all this and many other factors combined to drive the population of Paris to revolution on March 18, which unexpectedly placed power in the hands of the National Guard, in the hands of the working class and the petty bourgeoisie which had sided with it.

It was an event unprecedented in history. Up to that time power had, as a rule, been in the hands of landowners and capitalists, i. e., in the hands of their trusted agents who made up the so-called government. After the revolution of 18 March when M. Thiers' government had fled from Paris with its troops, its police and its officials, the people became masters of the situation and power passed into the hands of the proletariat. But in modern society, the proletariat, economically enslaved by capital, cannot dominate politically unless it breaks the chains which fetter it to capital. That is why the movement of the Commune was bound to take on a socialist tinge, i. e., to strive to over throw the rule of the bourgeoisie, the rule of capital, and to destroy the very *foundations* of the contemporary social order.

At first this movement was extremely indefinite and confused. It was joined by patriots who hoped that the Commune would renew the war with the Germans and bring it to a successful conclusion. It enjoyed the support of the small shopkeepers who were threatened with ruin unless there was a postponement of payments on debts and rent (the government refused to grant this postponement, but they obtained it from the Commune). Finally, it enjoyed, at first, the sympathy of bourgeois republicans who feared that the reactionary National Assembly (the "rustics", the savage landlords) would restore the monarchy. But it was of course the workers (especially the artisans of Paris), among whom active socialist propaganda had been carried on during the last years of the Second Empire and many of whom even belonged to the International, who played the principal part in this movement.

Only the workers remained loyal to the Commune to the end. The bourgeois republicans and the petty bourgeoisie soon broke away from it: the former were frightened off by the revolutionary-socialist, proletarian character of the movement; the latter broke away when they saw that it was doomed to inevitable defeat. Only the French proletarians supported *their* government fearlessly and untiringly, they alone fought and died for it - that is to say, for the cause of the emancipation of the working class, for a better future for all toilers.

Deserted by its former allies and left without support, the Commune was doomed to defeat. The entire bourgeoisie of France, all the landlords, stockbrokers, factory owners, all the robbers, great and small, all the exploiters joined forces against it. This bourgeois coalition, supported by Bismarck (who released a hundred thousand French prisoners of war to help crush revolutionary Paris), succeeded in rousing the ignorant peasants and the petty bourgeoisie of the provinces against the proletariat of Paris, and forming a ring of steel around half of Paris (the other half was besieged by the German army). In some of the larger cities in France (Marseilles, Lyons, St. Étienne, Dijon, etc.) the workers also attempted to seize power, to proclaim the Commune and come to the help of Paris; but these attempts were short-lived. Paris, which had first raised the banner of proletarian revolt, was left to its own resources and doomed to certain destruction.

Two conditions, at least, are necessary for a victorious social revolution - highly developed productive forces and a proletariat adequately prepared for it. But in 1871 both of these conditions were lacking. French capitalism was still poorly developed, and France was at that time mainly a petty-bourgeois country (artisans, peasants, shopkeepers, etc). On the other hand, there was no workers' party; the working class had not gone through a long school of struggle and was unprepared, and for the most part did not even clearly visualise its tasks and the methods of fulfilling them. There was no serious political organization of the proletariat, nor were there strong trade unions and co-operative societies....

But the chief thing which the Commune lacked was time - an opportunity to take stock of the situation and to embark upon the fulfilment of its programme. It had scarcely had time to start work, when the government entrenched in Versailles and supported by the entire bourgeoisie began hostilities against Paris. The Commune had to concentrate primarily on self-defence. Right up to the very end, May 21-28, it had no time to think seriously of anything else.

However, in spite of these unfavourable conditions, in spite of its brief existence, the Commune managed to promulgate a few measures which sufficiently characterize its real significance and aims. The Commune did away with the standing army, that blind weapon in the hands of the ruling classes, and armed the whole people. It proclaimed the separation of church and state, abolished state payments to religious bodies (i.e., state salaries for priests), made popular, education purely secular, and in this way struck a severe blow at the gendarmes in cassocks. In the purely social sphere the Commune accomplished very little, but this little nevertheless clearly reveals its character as a popular, workers' government. Night-work in bakeries was forbidden; the system of fines, which represented legalized robbery of the workers, was abolished. Finally, there was the famous decree that all factories and workshops abandoned or shut down by their owners were to be turned over to associations of workers that were to resume production. And, as if to emphasize its character as a truly democratic, proletarian government, the Commune decreed that the salaries of all administrative and government officials, irrespective of rank, should not exceed the normal wages of a worker, and in no case amount to more than 6,000 francs a year (less than 200 roubles a month).

All these measures showed clearly enough that the Commune was a deadly menace to the old world founded on the enslavement and exploitation of the people. That was why bourgeois society could not feel at ease so long as the Red Flag of the proletariat waved over the *Hôtel de Ville* in Paris. And when the organized forces of the government finally succeeded in gaining the upper hand over the poorly organized forces of the revolution, the Bonapartist generals, who had been beaten by the Germans and who showed courage only in fighting their defeated countrymen, those French Rennenkampfs and Meller-Zakomelskys, [tsarist generals, notorious for their brutal punitive actions during the 1905–07 Revolution] organized such a slaughter as Paris had never known. About 30,000 Parisians were shot down by the bestial soldiery, and about 45,000 were arrested, many of whom were afterwards executed, while thousands were transported or exiled. In all, Paris lost about 100,000 of its best people, including some of the finest workers in all trades.

The bourgeoisie were satisfied. "Now we have finished with socialism for a long time," said their leader, the blood thirsty dwarf, Thiers, after he and his generals had drowned the proletariat of Paris in blood. But these bourgeois crows croaked in vain. Less than six years after the suppression of the Commune, when many of its champions were still pining in prison or in exile, a new working-class movement arose in France. A new socialist generation, enriched by the experience of their predecessors and no whit discouraged by their defeat, picked up the flag which had fallen from the hands of the fighters in the cause of the Commune and bore it boldly and confidently forward. Their battle-cry was: "Long live the social revolution! Long live the Commune!" And in another few years, the new workers' party and the agitational work launched by it throughout the country compelled the ruling classes to release Communards who were still kept in prison by the government.

The memory of the fighters of the Commune is honoured not only by the workers of France but by the proletariat of the whole world. For the Commune fought, not for some local or narrow national aim, but for the emancipation of all toiling humanity, of all the downtrodden and oppressed. As a foremost fighter for the social revolution, the Commune has won sympathy wherever there is a proletariat suffering and engaged in struggle. The epic of its life and death, the sight of a workers' government which seized the capital of the world and held it for over two months, the spectacle of the heroic struggle of the proletariat and the torments it underwent after its defeat - all this raised the spirit of millions of workers, aroused their hopes and enlisted their sympathy for the cause of socialism. The thunder of the cannon in Paris awakened the most backward sections of the proletariat from their deep slumber, and everywhere gave impetus to the growth of revolutionary socialist propaganda. That is why the cause of the Commune is not dead. It lives to the present day in every one of us.

The cause of the Commune is the cause of the social revolution, the cause of the complete political and economic emancipation of the toilers. It is the cause of the proletariat of the whole world. And in this sense it is immortal.

5

Do you know Lefrançais?

DANIEL BENSAÏD

Less famous than Varlin, Vallès, Flourens or Rossel, he was never-theless the first president of the Paris Commune and, Frenchman though he was [a wordplay on his name], Eugène Pottier dedicated the Internationale to him.

Born in 1826 into an anti-Bonapartist family, he entered the Ver-sailles teacher training college in 1842, but was unable to find a post when he left: he was already banned from teaching because of his sulphurous views. After the temporary replacement of a colleague in Dourdan, where he had a run-in with the local priest, he had to resign himself to becoming a writing clerk for a Parisian contrac-tor, he was dismissed as soon as the February 1848 revolution be-gan. His life as a communist then becomes the exemplary chronicle of a militant in the century. Arrested even before the June days (the uprising of 22-26 June 1848), he was sentenced to three months in prison and two years of surveillance for possession of weapons of war, sent to Dijon under house arrest. Exiled to London in 1851, he could meet Marx, Mazzini and Louis Blanc between Dean Street and

Greek Street. He founded a cooperative restaurant, "La Sociale", before returning to Paris in 1853.

In the 1860s, he immersed himself in the grassroots activity of the clubs and meetings where the socialist movement was rebuilding its strength. Police reports consider him one of the most popular speakers of the time: "He develops his theories on collective property and the suppression of inheritance; he violently attacks the institution of marriage and advocates free union."

A member of the Vigilance Committee during the siege of Paris in 1870, Lefrançais actively participated in the riot of 31 October against the defeatist flabbiness of the "National Defence" government. Imprisoned for four months in Mazas, then in Vincennes and in La Santé, he was elected deputy mayor of the 20th arrondissement and acquitted by a war council on 24 February 1871. On 26 March, he was elected to the Commune by the 4th arrondissement. Fighting on the last barricades of the Bastille and the Arsenal, he managed to escape to Switzerland. The council of war sentenced him to death *in absentia* on 30 August 1872.

In Geneva, he joined the local section of the International and then its Jura "anti-authoritarian" federation, incurring the wrath of the "Marxists" who denounced his role "at the head of these lunatics". He participated in the presidency of the international anti-authoritarian congress of Saint-Imier in September 1872 and contributed to *La Révolution sociale*, the organ of the Jura federation influenced by Bakunin. Earning his living as a clerk, he assisted Élisée Reclus in his geography work, fought a duel, and returned to Paris after the amnesty in 1880. Having often denounced "the deception of universal suffrage", he agreed to be a candidate in the legislative elections of 1889, as an "anti-Ferry and anti-Boulangist" protest.

He died on 16 May 1901. At his funeral in Père Lachaise on 19 May, a companion read his will:

I am dying more and more convinced that the social ideas I have professed all my life and for which I have fought as hard as I could are just and true. I die more and more convinced that the society in which I have lived is nothing but the most cynical and monstrous of robberies. I die professing the deepest contempt for all political parties, even socialist ones, having never considered them to be anything but groups of simpletons led by shameless and unscrupulous ambitious men. As a final recommendation, I ask my son Paul to see to it that my funeral - exclusively civil, of course - be as simple as my life itself has been, and that I be accompanied only by those who have known me as a friend and have been kind enough to bestow upon me either their affection or more simply their esteem.

The citizen Gustave Lefrançais had known everything: misery, prison, exile, conspiracy, insurrection, and the death sentence. Without ever giving up. Between the massacres of June 1848 and those of the *Semaine sanglante* [Bloody Week, the final week and defeat of the Paris Commune], his life is an example of uprightness and fidelity to the cause of the exploited and oppressed.

His story sums up the experience of a century in which history broke in two. Can one imagine the depth of this break? The young defrocked Ernest Renan, who witnessed the massacre from his window, wrote to his sister Henriette on 1 July 1848:

> The storm has passed, my dear friend; but it will leave a long trail of destruction! Paris is no longer recognisable: the other victories had only songs and follies; this one has only mourning and fury. The atrocities committed by the victors make us shudder and take us back in one day to the time of the Wars

of Religion. Something harsh, ferocious and inhuman is introduced into the customs and language. The people of order, those who are called honest people, ask only for machine-gun fire and shooting; the scaffold is shot down, massacre is substituted for it; the bourgeois class has proved that it is capable of all the excesses of our first Terror, with a degree of reflection and selfishness in addition.

1,500 killed in action. 3,000 executions. 12,000 deported. Twenty years later, Flaubert was still shuddering:

When the prisoners approached a window, the national guards who were on duty would stick bayonets into the crowd at random. They were generally ruthless. Those who had not fought wanted to signal their presence. It was an overflow of fear. They were taking revenge on the newspapers, the clubs, the assemblies, the doctrines, everything that had been exasperating for three months. The aristocracy had the fury of the scoundrel and the cotton hat showed itself no less hideous than the red hat. Public reason was disturbed as after the great upheavals of nature. People of spirit remained idiots for the rest of their lives.

And here [confirmed Lefrançais] are the sons of Voltaire, the old laughers of mystical relations, the eaters of priests, grouped around a pedestal table waiting for hours on end for this piece of furniture to lift its leg... Finally, religion in all its forms is on the agenda. It's very distinguished. France has gone mad. Madame Roland was right when she wrote that to me after 2 December.

Lefrançais and his brothers-in-arms were, on the contrary, denuded of this once and for all.

After June 1848, there was no longer one Republic, but two. Irreconcilable.

The blue and the red. The bourgeois and the social.

"And the real birthplace of the bourgeois republic is not the February victory; it is the June defeat." wrote Marx [in The Civil War in France]. "What relationship exists," Lefrançais asks again, "between the modern conception of an egalitarian republic, based on labour, and the ancient republics of patricians, plebs and slaves?" Decidedly, "our republic has nothing in common with yours": "June has sufficiently demonstrated this!"

About fifteen thousand men dead or wounded on both sides; the organized manhunt; one part of Paris denouncing the other; the fiercest hatreds unleashed between the army, the mobile and the workers, whose wounded inveigh against each other even on their hospital beds; the indefinite state of siege; the permanent councils of war to send the most energetic barricade fighters to gaol or even to the scaffold: such is the balance sheet of four months of government by the Republicans. What could the most execrable of monarchies have done?

Republican bullets from June 1848 or monarchist bullets from June 1832, it is all the same to those who receive them, "except that in 1848 there were more of them".

The lesson had been learnt. It would leave deep traces of popular hostility towards the democrats and bourgeois politicians, towards the hugolant Hugos and the gambetta-like Gambettas, always ready to turn against the "scoundrel" who serves as their footstool:

> Since his entry into the prefecture of police, on the evening
> of 24 February, hasn't Caussidière helped, along with Ledru-
> Rollin and Louis Blanc, to play into the hands of the reac-
> tionaries by stirring up the spectre of Blanqui. Why weren't

he and his friends present at the barricades, giving the movement the guiding impulse it lacked to concentrate its efforts
on the Assembly which should have been stormed from the
first day? It is this absence of direction which confines the insurrection to its quarters where the energy of the combatants
is spent in pure waste. Cavaignac and his friends understood
this well. So, soon reduced to the defensive, the insurgents
would remain insurgents - that is to say, defeated

Lefrançais noted in February 1848. The political experience is
also military: the art of insurrection is a war of movement and rapid
decision. Immobility and hesitation are synonymous with defeat. A
certain Lenin remembered this, half a century later, in those October days when he urged the leaders of his party to take action without delay: it was a matter of life and death.

The Commune of 1871 confirmed June 1848. The revolution
of 18 March brought to power a government of uneducated people,
"unknowns, ignorant people", who would one day be the glory of
"the first truly popular of our revolutions".

After the defeat, Lefrançais summarized the roots of the class di-
vide which was the key to the civil war:

> The real "crimes" of the Commune, oh bourgeois of all stripes
> and colours: monarchists, Bonapartists, and you too, pink
> or even scarlet republicans; the real crimes of the Commune
> which, to its credit, you will never forgive it for, I will enumer-
> ate them [...]. The Commune is the party of those who had
> initially protested against the war in July 1870, but who, see-
> ing the honour and integrity of France compromised by your
> cowardice, tried the impossible to ensure that the invader was
> pushed back from the borders [...]. The Commune, for six

months, defeated your work of treason [...]. The Commune demonstrated that the proletariat was prepared to manage itself and could do without you [...]. The reorganization of the public services which you had abandoned is clear proof of this [...]. The Commune has tried to substitute direct action and unceasing control by the citizens for your governments, all of which are based on "national interest", behind which your plunder and governmental infamies of all kinds take cover... Never, no never, will you forgive it.

The Commune, however, sinned by naivety in not understanding that "one cannot be both legal and revolutionary (on pain of falling between the two)". Lefrançois thus agrees with Marx that not having taken possession of the Banque de France constitutes "an irreparable fault".

Such Memoirs contribute to a better understanding of certain constitutive features of the French workers' movement. They shed light on the origins of revolutionary syndicalism, its tenacious mistrust of parliamentarianism, its workers' or populist accents, which the Communist Party was able to exploit to its own ends, in the inter-war period, in the service of Stalinist Bolshevization.

Proclaiming his communist convictions, a fighter like Lefrançais was nevertheless wary of populism from above and of the "exaltation of the workman's blouse" which had become "the catchphrase of the republicans of tomorrow". He mocks the "self-proclaimed friends of the people": "Do we need to proclaim that we love ourselves?"

Producers, let's save ourselves! For him, this formula is quite literal. It is the basis of his hostility to all forms of representative delegation and his undiminished taste for direct democracy. Twice in a quarter of a century, Lefrançais's generation had suffered the bitter ordeal of bourgeois cowardice and cruelty. Thus he (along with Val-lès, Varlin, Courbet, Franckel, Beslay, Longuet, Vermorel) belonged to the minority of the Commune which voted against the creation of a Committee of Public Safety. Not only did he disapprove of re-enacting the great hours of the Jacobin Terror as a farce, but he feared that such a committee would become a weapon in the hands of a party, whereas the Paris Commune was "the expression and im-personal force of the revolution". It must remain so.

As soon as it entered the Hôtel de Ville, the Central Committee declared that "the revolution of 18 March has first of all the aim of restoring to Paris, and consequently to the whole of France, the ef-fective sovereignty once more usurped by the people of 4 September [date of the declaration of the Third Republic in 1870]". It did not see itself as a Power, but as "a provisional instrument of popular sov-ereignty which immediately invites the population to elect its repre-sentatives". From then on, "the state would be the simple expression of communal interests in solidarity".

This vigilance against any form of delegation, confiscation or usurpation of power, and against the formation of a "new caste of state employees by means of a School of Administration" (an Ecole Nationale d'Administration before its time, envisaged by the Ther-midorian Carnot) was matched by a lifelong concern for educa-tion and popular organization. Lefrançais was constantly listening to what was brewing in clubs and associations. He marvelled at this proliferation of popular life and culture, where the working classes were learning on a large scale, in contrast to the closed circles of the secret societies. In the 1860s, he enthusiastically witnessed the rise of a modern workers' movement whose forms of solidarity clashed with the competition on which "the exploitation of wage earners by wage earners" was based. But he also fought against the Proud-honian illusions whose societies, "however fraternal they may be", would only "substitute the war from group to group for that from individual to individual". The only way to avoid this trap is "the federation of workers' associations in solidarity; but the idea is not yet ripe...".

Having begun his career as a teacher, Lefrançais remained particularly sensitive to educational programmes and methods. A few years later, he could have been a pioneer of the *Ecole émancipée* [a longstanding radical tendency in French teacher unionism, founded in 1910] and of teacher unionism. A member of the Association of Socialist Teachers, he contributed in the 1840s with a few friends, including Pauline Roland and Jeanne Deroin, to the development of an innovative programme under the Second Republic. During the Second Empire, while the workers' movement was getting its breath back, he joined a Scottish-rite Freemason lodge, but left immediately, scalded by "the most insipid and religious of the charitable societies".

On the other hand, it is striking to note how far removed from the narrow trade unionism confined to the closed horizon of the factory were these semi-legal meetings where the popular movement took on a new lease of life. The broad audience was curious about everything. It was passionate about the cause of women and about family and inheritance issues.

In 1849, invited to a meeting on education which did not look good, Lefrançais decided to stay when he saw "these ladies enter, convinced that the interest of the meeting would be affected by their presence". In 1868, one of the very first public meetings at the Vaux-Hall, attended by more than 2,000 people, mostly male and female workers, dealt with "women's work". The discussion concluded with a vote of principles "recognising the right of women to maintain their personality and hence their social equality through work."

The meetings debating the family were crowded. Between supporters of legal divorce and those of free union, the audience was often divided, but it did not matter: "The idea of free union was established." At the meetings at the Pré-au-Clercs, where the audience was mainly students, there was much discussion of marriage, heredity and the reciprocal rights of father and child. At the Folies-Belleville, where the "working class element" dominated, discussions were held mainly between socialist schools:

> The audience is very impressionable, easy to move and yet very attentive, there is nothing more interesting for the speaker than to see this ocean of heads reflecting the various emotions he himself has gone through and which he has been able to transmit to them.

The duplicity shown by the bourgeois Republic, on the other hand, had sown a stubborn suspicion about the claims that seem to be associated with it. Thus, Lefrançais was indifferent, even vaguely hostile to the idea of women's suffrage: what does it matter, he says, to the woman who gets her fingers bloody making artificial flower stems, or who ruins her health at work, to be able to be an elector and eligible. He also refused to be part of any society for the abolition of the death penalty, which already appeared to be the hobbyhorse par excellence of reformers who had given up on any other radical social reform and who did not hesitate to use the troops against the barricades:

> As long as thousands of workers have their heads, arms and legs cut off, their stomachs gutted by industrial machinery, for the greater satisfaction of the god Capital, I reserve my tears for them. The suppression of the death penalty incurred every

day in the factory by the exploited of big industry seems to me much more urgent than that of the penalty inflicted by the judges. Let's abolish the former first; the latter will logically follow.

Paul Lafargue had the same view. Here we can see at its source a workerism or a "pure socialism", whose legitimate distrust of bourgeois parliamentarism is transformed into a withdrawal from politics in general. The initial indifference of Guesdist socialism towards the Dreyfus affair, conceived as a settlement of accounts within the military caste and the ruling class, is part of this nascent tradition.

Parliamentary decay, the "elites" mixing with riff-raff, corruption and scandals are likely to revive this sensitivity today, which is sometimes dormant but deeply rooted in French popular culture. It is easy to understand, when reading these memories, that Lefrançais had a stormy temper. He was not easy to get along with and often ill-tempered. A tumultuous life tempered his character. Controversies and rivalries raged in the nascent socialist movement. The vigour of the confrontations does not, however, give the impression of the rancid and hardened sectarianism that ravaged the ranks of the workers' movement after the social-democratic assassination of Rosa Luxemburg and the introduction of Stalinist police methods.

Thus, everything opposes Proudhon and Leroux. The former is an individualist, the latter a communist. The former is an atheist, the latter a Christian. But both deserve respect, because they want to substitute solidarity and justice for the "every man for himself" of the bourgeois economists. Both have been compositors, proofreaders. They are "workers, proletarians, of great knowledge, able to discuss competently with the most learned specialists of the time".

Lefrançais, who had often fought against Proudhon, remembered his funeral with emotion. A crowd of five to six thousand people gathered in January 1865 for the funeral. A regiment approaches and returns to the barracks after a manoeuvre. It is thought to be a trap. They explain themselves. They negotiate. The ranks open up to let the troops through. An anonymous voice shouts: "Beat the drum!" The colonel raises his sword, heads are uncovered, and the regiment marches in front of the house of the deceased, presenting arms: "A deep emotion seizes everyone. We shook hands in silence. Not a shout, not a word in this crowd dominated by a feeling of dignified pride. We feel alive again. So not everything is dead."

Blanqui enjoyed a special respect in his eyes, as in Marx's by the way. Under Louis-Philippe, his Société des saisons was already distinguished. One "hardly laughs there", certainly, but one does not declaim there either. And every line carries. Marx said that the bourgeoisie invented the name of Blanqui to criminalize communism. Lefrançais sees in it the symbol of "the true Republic" whose time has not yet come.

Before the Bourges court, unlike Raspail who sought to justify himself, Blanqui, threatened with capital punishment, "widened the debate, tore off the veil of the supposed respect due to the majesty of universal suffrage and clearly demonstrated that it is the Revolution alone that is in the hot seat. As for his person, Blanqui has no concern about it. Not believing that a dictatorship, however enlightened, could bring about the triumph of the social revolution, Lefrançais could not be a Blanquist. He nonetheless proclaimed to the end, towards Blanqui "whose whole life has been generously sacrificed without reserve to the Revolution", the "respect to which he is entitled". He is more reserved towards the Blanquists.

More significantly, Lefrançais considered the arrest of Rossel for military incompetence by decision of the Commune to be legitimate. However, he specified: "As for believing him to be a traitor, nothing justifies such an opinion. He is a man who made a mistake."

Unlike what happened under the Robespierrist Terror, for him a mistake was neither a crime nor treason. Unlike the murderous rhetoric of the Moscow trials, Lefrançais ignored the infamous formula of "objective guilt".

Invited under the Republic of September 1870 to raise a toast to that of 1792, Lefrançais raised his glass to "those who fell in June 1848 for the conquest of social equality". Arago was in a tizzy. The young people, led by Flourens, applauded. There was no need, then, to invoke the duty of remembrance in order to be faithful. Lefrançais was not the type to commune with the "republicans of the two shores", from Pasqua to Chevènement. He will never be a black hussar [dogmatic school teacher] of the Republic. A red hussar, rather. Or even a black and red hussar. For he has a frankly libertarian communism.

He was made of the stuff that stiff-necked rebels are made of. We cannot imagine him being bogged down in the decorum and propriety of a governing, pluralist left. He already speaks with disdain of "the open left" as well as the "pink Republic". Different times, different customs? Maybe.

Times change, of course. But there remains a popular righteousness, whose first imperative was always to betray the bourgeoisie for the man.

Contrary to what my surname might indicate, my maternal grandfather, answering to the valiant first name of Hyppolyte, was born in 1861, at 1 passage de la Main-d'Or, into a family of cabinetmakers from the faubourg Saint-Antoine [in Paris]. After the crushing of the Commune, he had to follow his proscribed parents. Grandfather Hyppolyte had tears in his eyes when he mentioned a German called "Karle Marx" (sic!), of whom he had probably never read a line. In the family dining room, a portrait of Jean-Baptiste Clément was displayed. Every year, on the anniversary of the Bloody

Week, the table had to rise solemnly to sing *Le Temps des Cerises*. In times of sinuosity and flexibility, of repentance and reversals, when by dint of bending and bowing, we would end up crawling, may the rough stiffness of the forty-eighters and the communards encourage us not to bend and not to give in. As the song says: "All this does not alter the fact, Nicolas, that the Commune is not dead!" [in reference to a song "Elle n'est pas morte – Aux survivants de la Semaine sanglante", written about the Commune by Eugène Pottier].

The final word, of course, goes to Lefrançais, irreconcilable communist and irreducible rebel:

> Today, the Republic is only worth as much as it is the negation of all supremacy, of all privilege, not only of an administrative nature, but also and above all of an economic nature. In a word, the modern Republic is social. The great honour of the Paris Commune is to have understood this. And let the proletarians not forget that the latter [the more or less radical and even intransigent republicans] are no less dangerous among their implacable enemies. We are a thousand leagues away from the priestly Republic, the pawn Republic, the Republic of order, discipline and inequality; a thousand leagues away from a Left servile to the owners, from its denials and its disavowals; from its reverences and its genuflections.

With Lefrançais, one is in good company. One simply feels at home.

6

All the more monstrous because they were women

AN INTERVIEW WITH MATHILDE LARRÈRE

What can we say about the role of women during the events of 18 March 1871 which marked the beginning of the Paris Commune? Can we draw a parallel with other revolutionary days where the place of women is often highlighted, like the march on Versailles on 5-6 October 1789, and the demonstration for International Women's Day on 8 March 1917 which started the Russian Revolution?

There were a large number of women on 18 March to prevent the soldiers from seizing the cannons of the Butte Montmartre, which can be explained quite simply because it was early in the morning and women got up first to look for water, fuel and so on. But there were also men - if only because the women raised the alarm - and in particular the *fédérés* [from the battalions of the National Guard of the different arrondissements which federated together to defend

Paris from the Prussians], who were all men inasmuch as the National Guard was closed to women. So, when the soldiers and the people fraternized on the Champ des Polonais, it was quite mixed. On 5-6 October 1789 [during the French Revolution] women were the driving force (it was a corporation of women, the Dames de la Halle, which launched the movement), before being joined by the National Guard; and on 8 March 1917, it was International Women's Day (this day has since then been fixed on 8 March). But, in these different cases, everything happened as if the role of women during these days was only retained in return for their being rendered invisible the rest of the time, whereas they were also present on 10 August 1792, during other events of the Commune, the Russian Revolution and so on.

Their presence is thus visible when linked to their social and domestic role, in particular taking care of food: on 5 October 1789 it was a revolt about wheat, it was bread that they went to seek in Versailles, even if ultimately it was the king they brought back; and on 8 March, 1917, for many women in St. Petersburg, those from the working-class neighbourhoods, it was less a demonstration for women's rights than a demonstration for bread and for peace. Their participation in revolutionary events should not therefore be restricted to these days, however inaugural.

Afterwards, they were not able to participate in the official institutions of the Commune. Did they demand to do so?

The right to vote for women was not considered in electing the Commune on 26 March, and in fact there was relatively little demand for it. The right to vote was not a primary demand of women at the time: they had many others, and this is even more true of female participants in the Commune, who for the most part were socialists or "Montagnardes" (social democrats), but we will come back to their demands. It was the same thing during the French Revolution: we talk a lot about Olympe de Gouges and her Declaration of the Rights of Women and Citizens, which is a way of demanding the right to vote (without ever saying it explicitly), but the work of Dominique Godineau on revolutionary women shows that they asked much more to be able to join the National Guard than for the right to vote.

Was the participation of women in the fighting something specific to the Commune?

No, women have always been in combat, but we have to clarify what it was about. Fighting with arms in hand was more limited for women in the revolts before the Commune, if only because women did not necessarily know how to use guns, and because there was a weight of the mentality which made it impossible to imagine that women could kill when they give life. So they were kept away from the rifles. On the other hand, they took part in the barricade fighting (in particular in 1830 and 1848).

The barricade is there to obstruct a street, and the soldiers rush into the street and are stranded. The fighting then takes place in two dimensions: on the one hand, there is a face to face between the soldiers and the barricade (on which there are armed men), and, on the other hand, the people throw various objects from the windows - and in many cases this was women. This second dimension is just as important (those studying law enforcement during the July Monarchy riots note that there were more skull fractures than gunshot wounds), but it is often overlooked. In addition, women reloaded the guns, treated the wounded, supplied the barricades and so on. The specificity of the Commune is that women more often participated in the fighting with weapons in hand, especially on barricades abandoned by male combatants.

One of the significant women's organizations during the Commune was also linked to the fighting: the Women's Union for the Defence of Paris and Aid to the Wounded. Can you say a few words about it? What other types of settings could women organize themselves in?

Yes, this was an organization created by Élisabeth Dmitrieff, who was the envoy of the IWA [International Workingmen's Association, official name of the First International], from London to Paris. Originally there were two men who had to leave, but one of them could not leave because he was ill, and she replaced him at short notice.

This organization is interesting in its two aspects: the defence of Paris, which corresponds to the transgressive demand of women to be able to bear arms; and care for the wounded, which, on the contrary, falls under the traditional role of women in the gendered distribution of tasks. It was the most structured organization and was quite centralized, with three levels: local committees by arrondissements, in which representatives were elected constituting a committee, and finally an executive commission headed by Elisabeth Dmitrieff.

But other organizations existed, clubs in particular, such as the Montmartre club, in which André Léo participated. There were, moreover, certain tensions between these organizations: for example, when André also joined the Women's Union for the Defence of Paris and Aid to the Wounded, this dual membership greatly irritated Élisabeth Dmitrieff. These different executives were "women only" (even if the term is anachronistic), directed and organized by women, just like the women's clubs during the French Revolution or in 1848 (as well as the newspapers in 1848) although in some cases men could help. Women understood that this is how they should organize themselves in order to be able to act and be heard!

Can we name other famous female participants?

Apart from Louise Michel, all of them are largely forgotten. And if we remember Michel and, to a lesser extent Brocher, it is mainly thanks to their writings. Yet many other figures deserve to be known. For example, André Léo, author of a major text, "La guerre sociale", in which she denounces the desire, for a century, "to make a revolution without women"; Dmitrieff, who has disappeared and about whom we know very little after the Commune; Paule Minck; or even Nathalie Lemel, a little better known, close to Eugène Varlin, who before the Commune had created an important workers' and popular cooperative canteen, La Marmite.

But for most of the *communeuses*, we have few documents, apart from a few names on posters or the records of their trials in Versailles. That being said, even if they are a little more so than women, the male *communeux* are also relatively unknown, with the exception of Vallès, Courbet, Pottier and so on.

Besides entry into the National Guard and more generally the right to bear arms, what significant demands were made by women during the Commune?

They demanded what the women of 1848, to whom they were quite close socially and through political training, were already demanding: the right to work, and to be paid the same wages and therefore the same recognition of qualifications as men. They also demanded the right to education, the right to divorce, the recognition of "illegitimate" or "natural" children, the recognition of concubines (that they have the same rights as married women), and some, notably Louise Michel, demanded the abolition of prostitution.

Which of these demands were met?

Within the Women's Union for the Defence of Paris and Aid to the Wounded, there was a lot of thinking about women's work, and Élisabeth Dmitrieff managed to wrest promises of equal pay, and there was even a decree, for a particular profession [school teachers], guaranteeing equal pay; it even established cooperatives of producers (of women therefore). For instruction, many schools for boys and girls were opened. Concubines were recognized, since the

Commune decreed that the wives or concubines of National Guards wounded or killed in combat could receive a pension; and there was also a recognition of natural children. On the other hand, women were not accepted into the Federated National Guard: they took up arms themselves during the *Semaine sanglante*.

What was the place of women in the labour movement at the time?

It was very difficult. Not only was the labour movement dominated by men, but a number of currents were against women working, which they considered unfair because women were paid less. And they began to see them - even if this would be more the case later - as strike-breakers, which is not confirmed in the sources available since the division of labour was so gendered that a woman was not going to perform a man's job.

They also considered factory work to be unethical, and there were many within the labour movement and the International who wanted women, especially married women, to return to the home, even if it meant working from home, that is to say in even worse conditions than in the factories. In the French labour movement, there is added to this the weight of Proudhonism, and the deep misogyny of Proudhon.

This was certainly not the case for all activists. For example, Eugène Varlin was very much in favour of equality between men and women and in particular equal pay, and when he founded La Marmite with Nathalie Lemel, she had the same organizational role as him. But they were minorities: there were several congresses or conferences of the International before the Commune - notably during the universal exhibitions - which ended with texts that were deeply misogynistic and opposed to the work of women. It was against this that Dmitrieff, André Léo and Paule Minck fought before the Commune: they gave very well attended lectures where they defended the right to work and equal pay. The slogan "equal pay for equal work" is a slogan of the Paris Commune.

Can we speak of a feminist movement in France at the time?

It is difficult, because the Second Empire had largely crushed the feminist movements which had been able to form in 1848. It was reborn slowly, around these figures like André Léo or Paule Minck, but also Maria Deraismes, at the head of the newspaper *Le Droit des femmes* founded in 1869, and which played an important role in the *Association pour le droit des femmes* created in 1870.

But it was especially within the labour movement that a socialist feminism, or a feminist socialism, organized itself. It was after this that a feminist movement developed outside the labour movement, around the suffragettes, with Hubertine Auclert and Marguerite Durand.

After the end of the Commune, did women suffer any specific repression from the Versaillais?

Yes, but it is ambivalent. On the one hand, more women than men benefited from dismissal of their cases, where it has for a long time been said that justice was more lenient with women. But, on the other hand, if we look at the people who were convicted, we notice that women had harsher sentences: 13 per cent of the women convicted were sentenced to death, against 0.9 per cent of men convicted; and 13 per cent were sentenced to forced labour and 13 per cent to deportation, while these figures are 2.3 and 11 per cent for men. Because they broke all the rule!

They were all the more monstrous in the eyes of the Versaillais because they were women: they transgressed the order of the sexes by leaving the place reserved for them at the time (the kitchen and the cradle) and entering politics - and obviously entering it by the revolutionary route.

This is how we can understand the figure of the *pétroleuse* through which female supporters of the Commune were stigmatized. From the first fires of the Commune, this stereotype is present: it is found in the Versailles press, iconography, and trials, which always tried to prove that they had started the fires (the Versaillais forgetting that they were the ones who sent the first firebombs!).

Did the defeat of the Commune have negative consequences for the situation of women and their demands in the years that followed?

Not particularly. There was the restoration of "moral order" by the Versaillais, but it affected everyone, it was not unique to women. And when the Third Republic was established, it certainly excluded the right to vote for women, but because women were considered too *cléricales* [under the influence of priests], without this having a direct link with the Commune. There was therefore no "backlash" as there was after the French Revolution with the promulgation of the Civil Code (1804). The advances obtained were suppressed, one after the other, but this is true of all the work of the Commune, which has been erased.

7

Genderquake: Socialist women and the Paris Commune

JUDY COX

On 11 April 1871, three weeks into the life of the Paris Commune, a poster appeared on the walls of France's capital:

> Citizenesses, we know that the present social order bears within itself the seeds of poverty and of the death of all liberty and justice... At this hour, when danger is imminent and the enemy is at the gates of Paris, the entire population must unite to defend the Commune, which stands for the annihilation of all privilege and all inequality.

All women who were prepared to die for the Commune were urged to attend a meeting at 8pm at the Salle Larched, Grand Café des Nations, 74 Rue de Temple. Laundresses, seamstresses, bookbinders and milliners attended and there they established a new organization, the Women's Union. This Union was a part of the socialist First International, which had been established by Karl Marx and other socialists and trade unionists in London in 1864 with the aim of uniting workers across national borders. Within a few days, the Union became one of the most important organizations of the Paris Commune. Socialist women played an indispensable role in organising the working women of Paris to become Communards.

The Commune lasted only 72 days but in that short time it challenged hierarchies of gender which had been deeply entrenched for centuries. The role played by women in the Paris Commune attracted the attention of both contemporaries and historians. Images of unruly women populated contemporary accounts of the Commune. Historical studies of the Commune have tended to accept and even amplify a series of negative stereotypes that characterization working women as excitable, irrational and habitually violent. They are seen as outside any enduring feminist or socialist tradition.

The histories that treat women more objectively tend to restrict discussions of their activities to specific chapters, reinforcing the idea that men had historical agency but women were marginal to events. Imagine reading a history of the Commune with a chapter titled, "Men in the Commune". The female Communards have been the exclusive focus of only three book-length studies, one published in 1964, one in 1996 and one in 2004. This article does not aim to retell the stories of the female Communards, fascinating though they are. It aims to explore the impact of socialist women on the Commune and on the wider socialist tradition.

The foremothers of the Commune

Most studies of the Commune begin on 18 March with the failed attempt of Adolphe Thiers, head of the French government, to disarm the Parisian National Guard. France had suffered a military defeat in a war with Prussia, following the long and bitter siege of Paris. The French government had agreed to surrender, but the population of Paris and the National Guard resisted. When government troops were sent to take the cannons of Paris, thousands of women, men and children rose up to defend them, built barricades and drove the French army out of the city. The emphasis on this revolutionary moment creates the impression that the Commune was a purely spontaneous event. The Commune was indeed born out of this spontaneous rebellion, but it was shaped and driven forward by individuals and organizations steeped in experience of the labour and socialist movements.

The role of socialist women in preparing the way for the Commune has been almost completely overlooked by historians, yet the Commune depended on the women who were at the centre of Paris's working-class networks. Male and female members of the International established themselves by leading strikes in the 1860s. Eugène Varlin and Nathalie Lemel led a large strike of bookbinders in 1864. Lemel defied convention to become a member of the strike committee and she fought tirelessly for equal pay for women. Both Varlin and Lemel became leading Communards.

Two opposing traditions relating to women co-existed uneasily inside the French socialist movement. One went back to the utopian socialism of the 1830s, when Flora Tristan became the first reformer to argue that women could only win equality through the emancipation of the working class. This tradition was developed in the 1848 Revolution by the great socialist leaders Jeanne Deroin and Pauline Roland, who organized women to fight for their rights to work and to vote.

A very different tradition was represented by the misogynistic anarchist-socialist writer Pierre-Joseph Proudhon. Proudhon argued that women were physically weak, incapable of abstract thought and naturally immoral, fit only for marriage or prostitution. In his last work, *Pornocracy: Women in Modern Times*, Proudhon argued that husbands had the right to kill wives who were adulterous, immoral, drunk, thieving, wasteful or obstinately insubordinate.

Jules Michelet further popularized these misogynistic views in his accessible novels {*Love*} (1858) and {*Women*} (1859). Michelet blamed women for the failure of the revolutions of 1789 and 1848 and considered them to be prisoners of their biology, which left them unreliable, capricious and unsuited to work outside the home. Proudhon and Michelet were very influential in the French section of the International.

At the French section's inaugural meeting in 1866, delegates passed a motion that stated: "From a physical, moral and social viewpoint, women's work outside the home should be energetically condemned as a cause of the degeneration of the race and as one of the agents of demoralization used by the capitalist class". There were opposing voices, including those of future Communards Varlin and Benoît Malon, but the French section of the International remained deeply Proudhonist.

Female campaigners fought back against the sexist ideas of Proudhon and Michelet. One combatant was André Léo. Léo had lived in Switzerland with her husband, a utopian socialist who had been inspired by the ideas of Henri de Saint-Simon and was forced into exile after 1848. Léo was widowed and to survive she published several novels exploring the oppression of women and affirming women's abilities. In 1866 she hosted the inaugural meeting of a new feminist group at her house. The group included Paule Mink, Louise Michel, Eliska Vincent, Noémi Reclus and her husband Élie Reclus, all future Communards. The group established improving girls' education as their campaigning priority.

Mink and Michel were two of the leading women of the Commune. They both stood in the revolutionary socialist tradition of Deroin and Roland. Mink was the daughter of an exiled Polish nobleman. When her marriage broke down, she worked as a seamstress and language teacher. She also edited a radical newspaper and built a reputation as an orator in Paris's radical circles. At a public meeting in 1868, Mink challenged Proudhon: "By ceasing to make woman a worker, you deprive her of her liberty and, thereby, of her responsibility so that she no longer will be a free and intelligent creature but will merely be a reflection, a small part of her husband". Michel was the daughter of an unmarried servant. She trained as a teacher but refused to teach in state schools because it would have meant swearing an oath of loyalty to the French Empire. Michel came to Paris to further both her education and the revolution. She was one of the most courageous, determined and audacious women in the revolutionary tradition.

Some male members of the International supported the women against Proudhonism. In 1866, Malon wrote to Léo as a member of the International, assuring her that he was not, "forgetting about the emancipation of women and we receive new support each day. We have convinced almost the entire association of the idea; only the pontiffs of Proudhon remain unconvinced". The first edition of the paper issued by the Batignolles-Ternes section of the Parisian International included a programme, signed by Léo and 16 others, which declared: "It is time to have women participate in democracy instead of making them its enemy by senseless exclusion". The following year Varlin argued:

> Those who wish to refuse women the right to work want to keep them permanently dependent on men. No-one has the right to refuse them the only means of being truly free.

> Whether done by man or women, there should be equal pay for equal work.

Léo, Mink and Varlin consistently agitated for the International to support both civil rights for women and women's right to work.

Throughout the 1860s women joined the political clubs that attracted large audiences in Paris's poorer districts, at least some of which discussed how to campaign against women's low wages. The political clubs also incubated the desire, "to establish a commune based on cooperation of all energies and intelligences instead of government composed of traitors and incompetents". Early in 1869 demands for a commune could be heard in many clubs, and proceedings often closed with the cry, "Viva la Commune".

When the Commune became a reality two years later, the clubs continued to provide a space for debate and organization and became a living link between the Central Committee and the people. The clubs debated what actions the Commune should take and made their views and priorities known to the Central Committee. Through the clubs, women could organize direct action against profiteers and urge support for reforms they wanted. Many Parisian women were in relationships with members of the National Guard, but few went through a marriage ceremony. Only married women could claim a wives' allowance from the Commune, a discriminatory policy that caused much anger. The demand for allowances for the unmarried partners of national guardsmen originated in the clubs and was later granted by the Commune

Some clubs were mixed, some were segregated, and both provided a platform for female leaders to emerge. An English reporter from the *Daily News* described one club where "respectably dressed women with their grown up daughters, little shopkeepers' wives with their young families" mixed with "those repulsive females of almost all degrees of age who form the typical furies of excited Paris mobs". Reporters were horrified to hear women advocating not only an end to marriage but also for equality between the sexes. Michel presided over the Club of the Revolution, which voted to arrest any priests who were in league with the "monarchist dogs" and to set up corporations of women and men to undertake necessary public works. At the Club of the Free Thinkers, Nathalie Lemel and Lodoyska Kawecka, who dressed in trousers and wore two revolvers hanging from her sash, argued for divorce and the liberation of women. At the Club of the Proletarians a laundress, known only as Madame Andre, was the secretary. One regular speaker was a Citizeness Thiourt, who demanded that cannons be placed in the well-to-do squares of Paris and that women be given the right to bear arms. Léo, Michel and Lemel toured the clubs arguing that capitalist exploitation must be abolished.

Before the storm: women under siege

The year 1870 began with a huge political revolt in Paris. Emperor Louis Bonaparte's cousin, Pierre, murdered a Republican journalist, Victor Noir. The murder sparked outrage and many women joined the 100,000 who marched through Paris in protest. A wave of repression was unleashed against members of the International. In the summer, the emperor declared war on Prussia but within weeks French forces had been defeated. On 4 September 1870 news of the defeat reached Paris. Thousands surged onto the streets, the Second Empire was overthrown and a Government of National Defence was established. The new government, however, refused to represent the interests of those who had installed them in office. The government's attempts to surrender to the Prussian army sparked weeks of unrest led by Parisian workers and the National Guard, whose members were drawn from the working class.

On 18 September 1870 many women were in the streets demanding the right to take up arms in defence of the French city of Strasbourg, which was besieged by Prussian troops. Louise Michel and André Léo led a delegation of women, students and school pupils to the Hotel de Ville, where they were locked up for a few hours. On 19 September Prussian troops laid siege to Paris. Around 100,000 rich citizens fled and 200,000 refugees from neighbouring towns entered the city. "Vigilance committees" were set up. Michel refused to recognize the segregated nature of the vigilance committees and joined the men's committee. She later described how "no one was very much bothered by the sex of those who were doing their duty. That silly problem was over and done with." Necessity led to an erosion of gender discrimination.

Food supplies to the city were blocked and women protested against long queues and catastrophic food shortages. Women needed new ways to organize and socialist women were at the heart of creating them. Nathalie Lemel ran a cooperative restaurant called La Marmite. She was active in several of the many mutual aid groups which the police kept under surveillance because they had the potential to turn into resistance groups. La Marmite was based on solidarity between those working in supply, catering and production, bound together with a hefty dose of socialist propaganda. Victorine Brocher, another member of the International, ran a cooperative bakery in La Chapelle which donated a proportion of its funds to new cooperatives. Many more socialist women were at the centre of efforts to feed the people during the siege, efforts which placed them at the centre of mutual aid networks and political organization.

An attempted insurrection in Paris on 22 January 1871 demanded that the government be replaced by a Commune. Large numbers of women and national guardsmen massed on the streets of Paris. However, the failure of the insurrection led to a backlash and then on 28 January the French government officially surrendered to Germany.[1]

A general election held on 8 February was a massive defeat for the left with landowners, aristocrats and army officers forming the majority of those elected. The French section of the First International had 50,000 members in the spring of 1870 but after the February elections, leading members felt they were on the brink of collapse as support drained away. However, some glimpses of the insurgency to come were nevertheless visible. On 26 February, a rumour that German troops were planning to enter Paris in order to take the city's cannon brought a huge crowd of national guardsmen, women and children out to defend the cannon they had paid for with their subscriptions. Through all the turbulent events of 1870 and the first months of 1871, women were leading the crowds, urging defiance and creating the basis of the organizations which would create a workers' government.

The Universal Republic

The French government decamped to the safety of Versailles, on Paris's western fringes. On 18 March, Thiers, who had surrendered to Germany as the government's "chief executive", sent troops to disarm the Parisian National Guard. It was milkmaids who raised the alarm. The women of Paris swarmed among the government troops as they attempted to remove the cannon. Prosper Olivier Lissagaray, a socialist and a historian of the Commune, noted that "it was the women who were first to act". Women formed a human barricade between the government's soldiers and the National Guard. A government supporter, General Louis d'Aurelle de Paladines, described the significance of the women's actions:

> The women and children came and mixed with the troops. We were greatly mistaken in permitting these people to approach our soldiers, for they mingled among them and the women and children told them: "You will not fire upon the people." This is how the soldiers of the 88th, as far as I can see, and of another line regiment found themselves surrounded and did not have the power to resist those ovations that were given to them.

When the officer in charge, General Claude Lecomte, ordered the troops to fire on the crowd, they refused. Lecomte was taken prisoner and later shot.

Before March 1871, the Commune existed only as a political aspiration, a rallying cry and possible different future – but with the government gone and the army and police driven out, a real, living Commune based on the "anonymous power of Monsieur Tout-le-monde ('Mr Everyone')" was established. A great sense of freedom brought a mass movement of men, women and children exploding onto the streets. One witness described the atmosphere:

> There was, first of all, a grandiose festival, a festival that the people of Paris, the essence and symbol of the French people, and of humanity in general, created for itself and for the spring. Spring festival in the city, festival of the disinherited and the proletarians, revolutionary festival and festival of the revolution.

The revolution transformed all interactions: "The social life of the city was recalibrated according to principles of cooperation and association." All this energy and commitment was rapidly channelled towards running the vital services of the city.

Paris's state institutions had disintegrated or been destroyed by the government at Versailles. "All the respiratory and digestive apparatus of this city of 1,600,000 collapsed." The crisis was so deep that the cemeteries had ceased to bury the dead and some 300,000 were out of work. The General Council of the National Guard stepped up to take over running the state until elections were held. All foreigners were admitted to citizenship, all state functionaries either eliminated or paid a worker's wage and subject to immediate recall. Priests and nuns were despatched to private life. Manual workers and those from subordinate positions took over the jobs of the highly-paid bureaucrats and began to organize public services such as the post office.

The people of Paris transformed their physical environment, destroying the symbols of the old regime. On 10 April the guillotine was dragged to the Place Voltaire and publicly burned by a crowd led by women. On 16 May the Vendôme Column, which glorified Napoleon's imperialist conquests, was torn down and the square was renamed the Place Internationale. Communards tore down the symbols of the old order, but they also demanded positive change. The Commune had a policy of creating "communal luxury", a phrase coined by Eugène Pottier, who wrote the "Internationale" in order to commemorate the Commune "Communal luxury" was a programme for public beauty in which art would be integrated into public life rather than treated as a private commodity enjoyed by the wealthy. The radical painter Gustave Courbet worked for the Commune's Arts Commission. He described the enormous efforts people went to in order to reorder their society:

I have breakfast and preside over meetings for 12 hours each day. My head has begun to spin, but despite this mental torment, which I am not used to, I am enchanted. Paris is a true paradise! No police, no nonsense, no exaction of any kind, no arguments! Everything in Paris rolls along like clockwork. All the government bodies are organization federally and run themselves.

As art and politics became intertwined, female artists found their voice. Singer Rosalie Bordas, known as La Bordas, was born in Monteux in 1840 and learnt to sing in the Red Café, which was run by her parents. She moved to Paris and sang for the Paris Concert and in 1870, during the siege, she sang *La Marseillaise* and waved a tricolour on stage. She was committed to the Commune, performing revolutionary songs while wrapped in a red flag in order to raise funds for the wounded.

The Commune demonstrated that working class people were capable of organising society more efficiently and fairly than the privileged politicians and bureaucrats that they had replaced. However, many of the Commune's supporters had a wider ambition: to lay the basis of a socialist society. Elise Reclus, who had been a member of André Léo's feminist circle, wrote:

The Commune set up for the future a new society in which there are no masters by birth title or wealth, and no slaves by origin, caste or salary. Everywhere the word "Commune" was understood in its largest sense as referring to a new humanity, made up of free and equal companions, oblivious to the existence of old boundaries, helping each other in peace from one end of the world to the other.

They believed that the Commune could inspire an international movement towards egalitarianism and freedom.

Building a new society

Arthur Arnould published a book called *State and Revolution* in 1878, 40 years before Lenin's work of the same name. In it, Arnould explained the Commune's unique ambitions:

> The Paris Commune was something more and something other than an uprising. It was the advent of a principle, the affirmation of a politics. In a word, it was not only one more revolution. It was a new revolution, carrying in the folds of its flag a wholly original and characteristic programme.

To implement this programme required the mass involvement of the previously marginalized people of Paris. On 26 March, around 200,000 male Parisians elected a General Council to organize the Commune. When the results were declared, a third of those elected were members of the First International. The results were greeted with a "dazzling spectacle of hope for change, tens of thousands on the streets, *La Marseillaise* playing, red flags waving, seas of banners and bayonets glinting in the sun".

Women were not allowed to vote in these elections and their exclusion has prompted some historians to question whether women were really included in this "Universal Republic". Historian James McMillan argues that "it cannot be claimed that women's rights were at the top of the Commune's priorities". There are a number of reasons for this perception of the Commune. When the government troops were driven out of Paris, the Federation of the National

Guard filled the vacuum of power. Based on military service, it was an entirely male organization. The National Guard ceded power to the formal institution of the Commune that was the town council of Paris, albeit one which was rapidly adapting to the revolution taking place in the streets. The inheritances of the past shaped the formal structures of the Commune, even while the mass movement was establishing new priorities and aspirations. One such inheritance was the voting system used under the Second Empire that excluded women and reflected the entrenched nature of sexism in French society.

A further reason for the negative interpretation of the role of women in the Commune lies within feminist histories that equate feminism with a "vocabulary of rights" that limits definitions of feminism to the pursuit of equal civil rights for women. The female Communards rejected the idea of civil rights and instead demanded the right to work and to organize collectively. They did not present themselves in terms of civil rights and so have been overlooked in feminist histories of France.

The exclusion of women from the formal institution of the Commune might have been challenged if the Parisian Revolution had survived for more than a few weeks. There was constant debate about the role women should play in the Commune. André Léo complained that women who wanted to support the Commune were at times rebuffed by male militants who did not want women to act as nurses and supply the front lines. The Marxist wing of the First International was the only political organization in France which supported the female franchise. At least four socialist members of the Commune - Eugène Varlin, Benoît Malon, Édouard Vaillant and the Hungarian Leó Frankel - took initiatives that promoted women's equality in their areas of responsibility. One historian of the Commune, Gay Gullickson, argues that since no women were members of the Commune's leading bodies - the Central Committee, the Communal Council and the National Guard - the Commune could not represent their interests.

However, Gullickson's argument overlooks the ways in which the Commune did respond to female activism. Indeed, it was the first French regime to appoint women to positions of responsibility, where they led welfare programmes, made vital appeals for support to provincial cities and transformed education. Evictions were banned, and allowances for unmarried partners of national guardsmen and their children were introduced. Many contemporaries saw this as the Commune's most revolutionary measure. Communard Arthur Arnould wrote:

> This decree, which raises woman to the level of man, which puts her, in the eyes of morals and the law, on a footing of civic equality with man, placed itself upon the plane of living morality, and delivered a mortal blow to the religio-monarchical institution of marriage as we see it functioning in modern society.

Arnould was being a little optimistic in his assessment, but it was a move of great significance for working-class women. Other important reforms included banning the sale of the many thousands of items left in pawn shops. The Commune also organized public assistance schemes, distributing tokens to the poor and setting up public canteens. In April, the Commune announced it was requisitioning the houses left empty by the rich for the use of poor families.

A second problem with Gullickson's argument is that she approaches the Commune from the top down rather than the bottom up. The militant women's organizations in the Commune and leading women activists such as Louise Michel did not see the vote as central to their vision of collective liberation. They tended to be dismissive of the right to vote and focused instead on the right to work and to bear arms, which they saw as more fundamental and immediate. They found ways to shape the Commune through organizing in their communities and workplaces, their unions, committees and clubs.

In its 72 days, the Commune did not completely uproot centuries of women's oppression. It did, however, both promote women to positions of authority and enable women to have real power over their lives. When assessing the Commune's record, it should be remembered that nowhere internationally, with the exception of one area of Australia, did even property-owning women have the right to vote in major elections in 1871. No women served in the French government until three women were appointed by the Popular Front coalition of 1936. These women were appointed rather than elected because they could not stand for office or vote in an election until 1945. Viewed from an international and historical perspective, the Commune stands out as a form of government that encouraged the active support of women.

In return, women made huge sacrifices to support the Commune. They had none of the time, freedom and energy bestowed by running water and toilets in their homes, by gas, electricity and public transport. They had to manage their periods, pregnancies and childbirth without basic hygiene, pain relief and medical support. They had little or no education, no health service and no pensions. In normal times they were seen as inert and resigned and in thrall to the Catholic Church. Yet during the Commune those women began to act as if they felt they would be listened to, as if they could make a difference. And make a difference they did.

On 1 April the government declared war on Paris. On 11 April the Union of Women for the Defence of Paris was established. It aimed to mobilize women to defend the Commune, treat the wounded and carry out important work. Its committees met daily in most districts of Paris and it became "the Commune's largest and most effective organization". The Union aimed to organize the defence of Paris's revolution and to instigate long-term changes in women's labour to eradicate the masters and exploiters. It issued an address calling on the Commune to abolish all forms of gender inequality and describing sex discrimination as a means employed by the ruling class to maintain their power. This was the first time a significant French women's organization explained their inferior status in terms of class.

The achievements of the Union were huge. It provided staff for orphanages and care for old people, recruited nurses and canteen workers, provided speakers for public meetings. The Union asked for space in local halls so it could meet and staff a desk providing information, aid and expenses for printing leaflets and posters - all of which the Commune provided. Nightly meetings of the Union were attended by between 3,000 and 4,000 women.

The driving force behind the Union was an outstanding revolutionary socialist leader, Elisabeth Dimitrieff. Dimitrieff had escaped from her native Russia for less repressive Geneva, where she was one of the signatories of the founding document of the Russian section of the International.

The document sought to synthesize Marx's economic theories with the beliefs of the influential writer Nikolai Chernyshevsky in the emancipatory potential of the traditional peasant commune. In Geneva, Dimitrieff met future Communards and supporters of women's rights, Eugène Varlin and Benoît Malon. Dimitrieff also edited a journal, {The People's Cause}. Its founding statement declared:

As the foundation of economic justice, we advance two fundamental theses:

The land belongs to those who work it with their own hands: to the agricultural communes.

Capital and all the tools of labour belong to the workers: to the workers' associations.

These ideas resurfaced in the Commune. Dimitrieff spent three months in London, discussing her journal with the Marx family. She requested to be sent to Paris and there she established the Women's Union. Dimitrieff 's politics shaped everything she did. She sought out working-class women, recruiting laundresses and seamstresses to the Union.

The Women's Union was not the only organization created by socialist women to support and influence the Commune. Beatrix Excoffon and Anna Jaclard were members of the Women's Vigilance Committee. Then there was Anna Korvin-Krukovsky, born in Russia to an aristocratic family. In the 1860s, the great Russian writer Fyodor Dostoyevsky had proposed to her but she rejected him. Anna and her sister, the mathematician Sophie Korvin-Krukovsky, escaped from Russia and managed get to France and Germany respectively.

Anna met Victor Jacland at a revolutionary meeting, and in 1869 the two were forced into exile in Switzerland. They returned to Paris when the Second Empire fell in 1870, and he was elected to the Central Committee of the National Guard. Anna helped to establish the Montmartre Vigilance Committee, which ran workshops, recruited ambulance nurses, sent women speakers to clubs and hunted down draft dodgers. It was another organization which enabled women to express their own aspirations and organize to achieve them.

How women shaped the Commune

To explore how women shaped the Commune, I will look at four key areas: women's work, women's education, women's attempts to spread the revolution and women's attitude to their new state.

Women's work

The Commune gave women work. Lissagaray saw 1,500 women sewing sandbags for the barricades, while another 3,000 worked on making cartridges. Benoît Malon and Leó Frankel were both members of the International and were also in charge of the Commission for Labour. They believed this commission was the most important mechanism for implementing lasting social change. Frankel explained:

> The people created its political organism as a mean of realising the very aim of the revolution, that is the emancipation of labour, the abolition of monopolies, privileges, bureaucracy, speculative, capitalist and industrial feudalism.

The Commission for Labour was shaped by and absolutely depended upon the Women's Union. On 16 April the Communal Council decreed that workshops whose owners fled to Versailles would be passed to the "cooperative association of workers who were employed there".

Dimitrieff believed that taking over the workshops was a way to transform labour by introducing equal pay, shorter working hours and ending the competition between women and men. Frankel and Malon drew up a plan for women's labour and put Dimitrieff in charge. She envisaged the workshops as free associations of labourers working for their collective profit:

> In taking work away from the bondage of capitalistic exploitation, the formation of these organizations would eventually allow the workers to run their own business.

The working class was not yet powerful enough to organize production collectively through workers' councils. Nevertheless, Dimitrieff, Frankel and Malon tried to separate labour from exploitation by workshop owners and instead direct it according to the needs of both consumers and producers.`

Education for emancipation

André Léo, Paule Mink, Louise Michel and Noémi and Élie Reclus had developed their ideas about female education in the 1860s. The Commune afforded them the opportunity to put their ideas into practice. The Commune's Education Committee included these veterans of the 1860s women's organization as well as Jaclard and Dimitrieff. The Education Committee was no moderate means by which women could extend their traditional domestic role into the public sphere. It was a tool for empowering women and enabling them to participate in the Commune while simultaneously subverting gender stereotypes. Despite the desperately limited means at its disposal, the Commune prioritized introducing education for girls. The radical newspaper *Le Père Duchêne* explained why:

> If only you realized, citizens, how much the revolution depends on women, you would have your eyes opened on girls'

education. You would not leave them, as has been done until now, in ignorance.

For many female Communards, education for girls was both a question of equality and of reforming human nature for a future socialist society.

Education became both free and secular. This meant turfing out nuns and priests and recruiting more teachers, with female teachers being awarded equal pay. The commission drew up plans to establish day nurseries. Parental and community engagement was another priority. Twice a week the Society for a New Education, which was composed of three women and three men, brought teachers and parents together to discuss the curriculum and the methods used in schools. The committee took a radical approach to education: "Any official direction which is imposed on the judgement of pupils is fatal and must be condemned... It tends to destroy individuality". Women did not just sit on committees. Mink opened a girls' school in the chapel of Saint-Pierre de Montmartre. Marcelle Tinayre, who was the first female school inspector in France, took charge of the secularization process in the 12th Arrondissement area of Paris.

Spreading the revolution

The Communards understood that the Paris Commune could not survive if it remained isolated from the rest of the country. After initial uprisings in other major towns were crushed, practical and political support from the small farmers around Paris was vital to feeding the city. Women were at the forefront of reaching out to the peasantry. Léo was largely responsible for writing a manifesto for rural workers, "To the Workers of the Countryside", although Malon also contributed to it. Some 100,000 copies were printed. "What Paris wants is the land for the peasants, the tools for the workers and work by and for everyone," Léo argued. What does it matter, she continued, if the oppressor is called a landowner or a manufacturer? The pamphlet pointed out that "if Paris falls, the yoke of poverty will remain on your neck and pass onto your children". Léo proposed ways that the capital could reach out to the rest of the country and Mink toured the provinces raising support. Léo and Mink were entirely right to direct their efforts towards winning support outside Paris. Marx argued that it was the Commune's isolation from the countryside that proved to be fatal. No press reports reached the small villages. Their inhabitants had no chance to see that the Commune represented their "living interests" and "real wants" without communication from the Communards.

Dimitrieff also urged the General Council to increase its efforts to break out of isolation, but she set her sights on other European nations rather than the countryside. She understood that the military forces were regrouping at Versailles, but believed that if the Commune could deepen its efforts at reform, it would also deepen its international support: "If the Commune is victorious, our political organization will be transformed into a social one, and we will create new sections of the International". Dimitrieff wrote optimistically to Marx, outlining how revolt might spread across Europe:

> In general, the internationalist propagandizing I am doing here, in order to show that all countries, including Germany, find themselves on the eve of the social revolution, is a very pleasing proposition to women.

According to Dimitrieff, women were particularly tuned in to the idea that the revolution must spread to countries such as Germany. Her strategy did not have the opportunity to become a reality.

Finishing the revolution

The Commune replaced the army and the police with the National Guard. Many radicals, including many women, wanted to use this revolutionary wing of the workers' state to overthrow the government at Versailles. However, Dimitrieff was one of the very few Marxists in the leadership of the Commune. Thus, discussions on whether to march on Versailles took place between Proudhonists who, as anarchists, did not believe in political action and Jacobins who were from a middle-class political tradition. The Blanquists were the main group to argue for the march on Versailles but they were too small to win wide support. On 2 April, Versailles launched an attack on a Parisian suburb. Women helped build new barricades and decided to lead an action of their own and launched an appeal in several newspapers:

> Let's go to Versailles. Let's tell Versailles what the revolution of Paris is. Let's tell Versailles that Paris has made the Commune because we want to stay free. Let's tell Versailles that Paris has made ready to defend herself because people tried to take her by surprise and disarm her. Let's tell Versailles that the Assembly is not the law, Paris is.

Beatrix Excoffon, known in her district as "The Republican", described the gathering on the following day:

I told my mother I was leaving, I kissed my children and off I went. At the Place de la Concorde, at half past one, I joined the procession. There were between 700 and 800 women. Some talked about explaining to Versailles what Paris wanted; others talked about how things were a hundred years ago, when the women of Paris had already gone to Versailles to carry off the baker and the baker's wife and the baker's little boy.

"The baker and the baker's wife and the baker's little boy" is a reference to the women's march on Versailles that took place in 1789. At that time, a hungry mob of women and men had laid siege to the Palace of Versailles and captured King Louis XVI and his family. Many female Communards invoked this militant revolutionary tradition of women's activism rooted in the Great French Revolution. However, unlike in 1789, the women's marches of 1871 were turned back by the National Guard, who feared the women would be shot by government troops.

Louise Michel was one of the most ardent supporters of a military attack on the government. She even volunteered to go to Versailles to assassinate Adolphe Thiers herself. She fought so bravely that the 61st Battalion gave her a Remington rifle and on receiving it she declared: "Now we are fighting. This is a battle. There is a rise, where I run ahead crying 'To Versailles! To Versailles!'" Michel instinctively knew that if the government at Versailles was not crushed, it would be unceasing in its efforts to overthrow the Commune.

After the defeat of the Commune, Paule Mink argued that the moderate minority in the Central Council lacked the courage to deliver a fatal blow against the government. In the face of the brutal suppression of the Commune, Mink drew the conclusion that centralized, organied revolution was the right strategy to achieve socialism. Lenin explored the experience of the Commune in his *State and Revolution* (1917) and raised the same criticism as Mink. He wrote that revolutions must:

> Suppress the bourgeoisie and crush their resistance. This was particularly necessary for the Commune; and one of the reasons for its defeat was that it did not do this with sufficient determination. The organ of suppression, however, is here the majority of the population, and not a minority, as was always the case under slavery, serfdom and wage slavery.

Michel, Mink and Lenin all made similar observations. The Commune had created a new kind of state, based on the engagement of the majority, but failed to direct its power against the old order, which would never stop seeking the means to destroy any hope of a different society.

Women on the barricades

On 21 May, troops sent from Versailles entered Paris and the entire population was summoned to the barricades. All contemporary accounts of the last days of the Commune pay tribute to the courage of women as they built barricades, nursed the wounded, supplied the National Guard with food and drink and fought alongside men. There was no great separation between nursing and fighting. Louise Michel described how women answered a call to volunteer to treat the wounded and often took up their rifles. André Léo noticed that officers were hostile to the nurses but the rank and file troops welcomed them. The Women's Union met on the same day that the government troops entered Paris. Nathalie Lemel, red flag in hand, led the women out to the barricade at Batignolles. Elisabeth Dimitrieff urged all devoted and patriotic women to organize the defence of the wounded.

Anna Jaclard and André Léo issued an appeal from their vigilance committee to the women of Montmartre, asking them to support a summons from the Commune: "The women of Montmartre, inspired by the revolutionary spirit, wish to attest by their actions to their devotion to the revolution." The women acted as ambulance nurses under fire and many were captured, raped and shot dead by the government troops. Fighting was a revolutionary act, which is why, as Edith Thomas pointed out, the same women who attended the political clubs were also those who climbed the barricades. The French government used brutal force to crush the Commune, with some 20,000 men, women and children executed during what became known as "Bloody Week".

Women were involved in all the military engagements during Bloody Week and many were listed among the wounded and the dead. One name on the list was that of Blanche Lefebvre, a laundress at the Sainte-Marie des Batignolles washhouse. She was a member of the Club of the Social Revolution, which had been set up on 3 May in the local church. Lefebvre was also a member of the Central Committee of the Women's Union. She was one of 120 women who held the barricade at the Place Blanche for several hours until they ran out of ammunition and were overrun. Those taken at the barricade were shot on the spot. Lefebvre was one of them. She was aged just 24.

The myth of the pétroleuse

It took the government troops seven long days of shelling, hand to hand combat and mass executions to retake Paris. Their revenge on women was particularly harsh. Women were systematically humiliated, stripped, raped and murdered by government troops. Malon attributed the troops' ferocity to lessons learned by the French army in its colonial subjugation of North Africa. Communards were shot where they were captured, but all working-class women were under suspicion. The women of the Commune were considered to have "unsexed themselves".

The *Times* reported that the women forgot "their sex and their gentleness to commit assassination, to poison soldiers, to burn and to slay". Opponents called female Communards evil, amazons, furies, jackals. The *Pall Mall Gazette* described the female Communards as, "hideous viragoes - furies intoxicated with the fumes of wine and blood". Wealthy society women lined up to abuse women prisoners and beat them with their parasols as they were dragged past on their way to prison. The myth of the "pétroleuse", women who burnt down buildings, began to circulate, justifying repression by dehumanizing its victims. Despite the myth, out of the 1,051 women who were arrested during the Bloody Week, only five were convicted of arson. Historians researching archives at the French Ministry of War have found, amidst the records of arrests, trials and pleas for clemency, evidence of the "dramatically varied way that women participated in the revolutionary struggle of 1871". These women were not protected by their sex: the state punished them precisely because they were women who refused to submit to oppression.

Dimitrieff escaped from Paris and sent a telegram from Geneva informing the International of her safe arrival. According to Lissagaray, Dimtrieff ran a hotel on the shores of Lake Geneva where she nursed refugees from the Commune. She then continued her agitation in Russia, turning towards political terrorism, perhaps as a result of her frustration at the defeat of the Commune. Malon, Léo and Mink also escaped to Geneva. Victor Jaclard was arrested and transferred to prison camp at Versailles but managed to escape and he and Anna also fled to Geneva. Thousands of others were not so lucky. Beatrix Excoffon was sentenced to transportation, although this was commuted to ten years in prison. Many thousands of other working women were summarily executed without a trial or imprisoned simply for expressing support for the Commune, for example, by allowing their shops to become meeting places.

Their stories illustrate the hopes that the Commune aroused among its supporters and how they experienced change in every aspect of their lives. A laundress named Marie Wolff was one of those prosecuted. On 27 May, four escaped prisoners who were supporters of the Versailles government were arrested. Wolff, who was an ambulance nurse, took part in their execution. Before the Commune, Wolff had served time in prison for theft and burglary. During the Commune she carried a red banner and a belt with weapons stuck in it. On 25 April 1872, Wolff was sentenced to death for her role in the execution of the prisoners. Her sentence was commuted to hard labour for life.

Marguerite Tinayre was a teacher and supporter of the International. Her husband, who was unpolitical, was shot as he searched for her. She was sentenced to transportation but escaped to Geneva and then Budapest with her five children. Tinayre was excluded from an amnesty of 1879 because she continued with her "socialistic and internationalist intrigues". She was eventually allowed back to Paris.

The revenge of the ruling class was brutal, but it did not crush the revolutionary spirit of the female Communards. Eliska Vincent, veteran of Léo's 1866 feminist group, was almost executed for her role in the Commune, but went on to lead a women's suffrage organization and edited a paper, *Equality*. Michel dared the court to sentence her to death. They declined and sentenced her to penal transportation. She met Lemel in the penal colony of New Caledonia in the South Pacific Ocean.

Michel returned to Paris after a total amnesty was declared in 1880. She was arrested on a demonstration of unemployed workers in 1883 and sentenced to six years of solitary confinement. She was arrested again in 1890 but escaped to England, where she taught refugee children. Michel returned to France and died of pneumonia in January 1905. More than 100,000 attended her funeral. When the Commune fell, Mink was touring the provinces to win support for the Commune. She managed to escape to Geneva with her daughter. She never stopped organizing for socialist revolution. When she was buried on May Day 1901, thousands of mourners joined the funeral procession through the streets of Paris, calling "Vive la Commune" and "Vive l'Internationale". Over 600 police, 500 soldiers and 100 cavalry were required to patrol the streets. Her funeral underlined the continuing importance of the Commune in the socialist tradition.

Conclusion: agitating and squawking

One historian of the Commune describes it as an "incubator for embryonic feminist socialisms". It would be more accurate to say that women's role in the Commune encouraged experienced socialist women to reach out to other working women. Mink wrote in the Geneva-based newspaper of the International, Equality, addressing women:

> It is in the name of women that I speak, in the name of women to whom the International has given the rights and

duties equal to those of men... Only socialism will be able to emancipate women materially and morally, as it will be able to emancipate all those who suffer!

Socialist men who supported women's emancipation were also keen to draw the lessons of the Commune. In 1871, just weeks after the defeat, Malon argued that "one important fact demonstrated by the revolution in Paris is the entry of women into political life... Women and the proletariat can only hope to achieve their respective liberation by uniting". At the same time, Leó Frankel wrote:

All the objections produced against equality of men and women are the same sort as those which are produced against the emancipation of the Negro race. Firstly, people are blind-folded and they are told that they have been blind since birth. By claiming that half of the human race is incompetent, man prides himself on appearing to be the protector of women. Revolting hypocrisy! Just let the barriers of privilege be lowered and we shall see.

In 1879, the national workers' congress in Marseille marked a decisive shift in attitude of organized French workers and a "majority rallied behind the notion of complete civil and political equality". The motion was ardently defended at the congress by Hubertine Auclert, a working-class socialist. She was acclaimed by the Congress, elected as chair of both the session and the commission, and the Congress adopted a resolution proclaiming the "absolute equality of the sexes".

The Paris Commune impacted powerfully on the Marx family. Marx initially opposed the Parisian uprising as premature. Yet once it was underway, he and the whole family threw themselves into supporting it. Marx was vilified as the "red doctor" and sinister insurrectionist who had instigated the Commune. Two of the Marx daughters, Eleanor and Jenny, were lucky to escape after visiting France in April 1871. Defeat brought refugees flooding into London and many found their way to the Marx family home. Jenny and the third sister Laura married Communards and Eleanor was engaged for a while to Lissagaray, whose invaluable history of the Commune she translated. The Commune also shaped the international socialist movement and was commemorated by the British working-class movement for decades with anniversary celebrations, speeches and events.

Marx described the Communards' greatest achievement as the new ways of organizing they created, the Commune's "actual working existence". The experience of 1871 prompted Marx to distance himself from the idea that revolutionary perspectives must be based on capitalist "progress". Rather, he saw non-capitalist forms of communal property ownership as creating potential allies for the working class. History progresses not through self-contained stages but rather through the interactions of town and country, worker and peasant. Despite its disastrous ending, the Commune was a new point of departure of world-historic importance. As Lissagaray wrote, the Commune was "the first attempt by the proletariat to govern itself". The only alteration Marx ever made to The Communist Manifesto was in 1872 when he added the line: "The working class cannot simply lay hold of the ready-made state machinery and wield it for their own purpose." For Marx, the Commune showed how the oppressive state could be broken and replaced with a democratic state run by the majority.

On the brink of the October Revolution of 1917, Vladimir Lenin drew on the experience of the Commune. He described how the abolition of the standing army and all officials being elected and subject to recall "signifies a gigantic replacement of certain institutions by other institutions of a fundamentally different type: democracy, introduced as fully and consistently as is at all conceivable, is transformed from bourgeois into proletarian democracy". When he defended the Bolsheviks from accusations that the party was too small to govern Russia, he argued that:

> We have a "magic way" to enlarge our state apparatus tenfold at once, at one stroke - a way which no capitalist state ever possessed or could possess. This magic way is to draw the working people, to draw the poor, into the daily work of state administration.

The Communards were the first to demonstrate this latent magic within the working class.

The Marxist analysis of the state is constantly under pressure from those who argue that the idea of "smashing the state" is outmoded and that many state-run services, such as health, education and welfare, must be preserved and extended rather than smashed up. The Communards did not "smash" the post office, the cemeteries or the schools; they took them over and ran them for the benefit of the majority.

As Lenin put it, the revolution must "cut the wires" that tie the useful aspects of the state from the capitalist interests that distort and limit them and from repressive institutions such as the police and army.

Rosa Luxemburg turned to the Commune in the last article she wrote, published in January 1919. She described how the Commune had ended in terrible defeat, like so many heroic working-class struggles. Then she asked:

Where would we be today without those terrible defeats, from which we draw historical experience, understanding, power and idealism? We stand on the foundation of those defeats; and we cannot do without any of them, because each one contributes to our strength and understanding.

The Commune was a working-class revolution that was necessarily also a "great gender event" because it depended on women's active involvement, creativity and courage. It was the visible involvement of women that made the Commune so appalling to its opponents. One wrote:

> Those females who dedicated themselves to the Commune - and there were many - had but a single ambition: to raise themselves above the level of man. They were all there, agitating and squawking, the gentleman's seamstresses, the gentleman's shirt makers, the teachers of boys, the maids of all work. During the final days all these bellicose viragos held out longer than the men did behind the barricades.

Across the English Channel, a *Times* reporter joined in the abuse, sneering: "If the French nation were composed only of the French women, what a terrible nation it would be." If the unruly women of Paris had been in charge of the whole country, it is conceivable that the revolution could have spread across Europe. Perhaps then, this brief but inspiring example of workers' power could have won more time and so provided us with many more examples of how working-class people can organize together to create a socialist society.

AN ODE TO EMANCIPATION

The author thanks Joseph Choonara, Richard Donnelly, Donny Gluckstein and Rob Hoveman for comments and suggestions.

Note

1. Germany had been formed just ten days earlier when, off the back of his military victories against the French, Prussia's King Wilhelm I was proclaimed headed of a unified German Empire at a ceremony in the Palace of Versailles.

8

Celebrating the Paris Commune of 1871: Glorious harbinger of a new society

SANDRA BLOODWORTH

Eleanor Marx wrote of the Paris Commune:

> It is time people understood the true meaning of this Revolu-
> tion; and this can be summed up in a few words... It was the
> first attempt of the proletariat to govern itself. The workers
> of Paris expressed this when in their first manifesto they de-
> clared they "understood it was their imperious duty and their
> absolute right to render themselves masters of their own des-
> tinies by seizing upon the governmental power.

Karl, her father, had addressed the International Workingmen's
Association (known as the First International) on 30 May 1871. He
began with: "On the dawn of March 18, Paris arose to the thunder-

burst of 'Vive la Commune!' What is the Commune, that sphinx so tantalising to the bourgeois mind?"

Marx went on to describe why he was so inspired. The Paris Commune

> was the first revolution in which the working class was openly acknowledged as the only class capable of social initiative, even by the great bulk of the Paris middle class – shopkeepers, tradesmen, merchants – the wealthy capitalist alone excepted.

Many of the lessons Marx drew from this momentous event have in the last half century been largely lost to workers struggling to get control over their lives. But if we listen to the voices of the women and men of the Commune, if we examine the barbarous response of the National Government headed by the reactionary Adolph Thiers, we find that the lessons are just as relevant to our struggle many years later. As Walter Benjamin argued so poetically:

> The class struggle, which always remains in view for a historian schooled in Marx, is a struggle for the rough and material things, without which there is nothing fine and spiritual... They are present as confidence, as courage, as humour, as cunning, as steadfastness in this struggle, and they reach far back into the mists of time. They will, ever and anon, call every victory which has ever been won by the rulers into question. Just as flowers turn their heads towards the sun, so too does that which has been turned, by virtue of a secret kind of heliotropism, *towards* the sun which is dawning in the sky of history. To this most inconspicuous of all transformations the historical materialist must pay heed.

In paying heed I will attempt to capture the incredible atmosphere of joy, experimentation and creativity which flourished. But we cannot flinch from the horror of that terrible last week, known as *la semaine sanglante*, where at least 30,000 people were slaughtered by a government determined to crush not just the physical presence of this social revolution, but also its spirit.

The preparedness of the ruling class to inflict such violence should be burned into the consciousness of every anti-capitalist activist. Any movement with a vision of a new society must confront the vexed question of how to win in the face of such barbarism.

The Commune established a more thoroughly democratic society than capitalism has ever seen before or since. The reforms introduced were far in advance of anything the capitalists had ever sanctioned, some of which still have not been won in many countries.

The 150th anniversary of this marvellous event is a good time to revisit the inspiring first steps of the revolutionary workers' movement, and draw the lessons that can be learnt from its successes and ultimate defeat.

The uprising

It all began as the sun rose over the radical working-class *arrondissements* [neighbourhoods] of Montmartre and Belleville on 18 March 1871. Soldiers began seizing nearly 250 cannon deliberately placed in these working-class areas by the National Guard, a popular Parisian militia. The soldiers had been sent there by the head of the new republican government, Adolphe Thiers. Among other things, Thiers was widely despised for his role in the brutal suppression of workers' rebellions in 1848.

But contrary to Thiers' expectation of a swift exercise, the affair spun out of control. The incompetent army had forgotten to bring horses to drag the cannon, which gave the Guardsmen time to fraternize with soldiers. Expecting a treasonous crowd, the soldiers began turning their rifles up as the streets rang with declarations of *Vive la République!*

The London *Times* correspondent describes the scene as women came out to buy bread and prepare for the day: "Small savage groups of blouses [were] making cynical remarks upon everybody's cowardice... 'If they had only left them to us to guard they would not have been captured so easily'." This militancy and self-assurance of the working women of Paris, convinced that they could fight better than the men, will reverberate through the whole revolution. Our witness, moving along to the suburb of Belleville, recorded soldiers and Guardsmen finding they had much in common. Let's pause to witness a typical scene:

> There was something intensely exciting in the scene. The uncertainty for a moment whether the men were meeting as friends or enemies, the wild enthusiasm of the shouts of fraternization, the waving of the upturned musket, the bold reckless women laughing and exciting the men against their officers, all combined to produce a sensation of perplexity not unmingled with alarm at the strange and unexpected turn things were taking.

Fraternization, courageous defiance by the masses of Paris and mutiny were the hallmark of the day. When troops blocked the entrance to the church of Saint-Pierre to stop anyone ringing the tocsin in order to alert the National Guard and citizens to the danger, workers got into other churches, climbing into the steeples. The tolling of the tocsins brought increasing numbers crowding into the streets.

The correspondent described these areas as "rugged open spaces where the lawless crowds of these parts love to hold their meetings and park their cannon". Belleville, side by side with Montmartre on the right bank, is described as "[t]he most solidly working-class district in all of Paris, and the most revolutionary". These cannon were regarded as *their* cannon, financed by workers' subscriptions to the National Guard since the revolution of 1848. And they were the only means of defence against the Prussian army shelling the city since Thiers had moved his troops to Versailles. When the *Times* correspondent queried a National Guardsman about possible fighting, he was rebuked: "*Sacrebleu*, do you suppose we are going to allow these *Canaille* to take our cannon without firing a shot?" After all, the National Guard had deliberately positioned their cannon to defend these key suburbs.

Hostile crowds quickly gathered to block the soldiers trying to move the cannon. Eyewitness accounts all draw our attention to the large numbers of women and children. Louise Michel, one of the most flamboyant and radical figures of the Commune, later recalled the events at Montmartre:

> Montmartre was waking up; the drum was beating. I went with others to launch what amounted to an assault on the hilltop. The sun was rising and we heard the alarm bell. Our ascent was at the speed of a charge, and we knew that at the top was an army poised for battle. We expected to die for liberty.

It was as if we were risen from the dead. Yes, Paris was rising from the dead. Crowds like this are sometimes the vanguard of the ocean of humanity... But it was not death that awaited us... No, it was the surprise of a popular victory.

Between us and the army were women who threw themselves on the cannons and on the machine guns while the soldiers stood immobile.

General Lecomte three times ordered the soldiers to fire on the crowd. "A woman challenged the soldiers: 'Are you going to fire on us? On our brothers? On our husbands? On our children?'" Lecomte threatened to shoot any soldier who refused to do just that. As they hesitated, he demanded to know if they "were going to surrender to that scum". Michel recalled:

> [A] non-commissioned officer came out from the ranks and...called out in a voice louder than Lecomte's. "Turn your guns around and put your rifle butts up in the air!" The soldiers obeyed. It was Verdaguerre who, for this action, was shot by Versailles some months later. [The government is often referred to as Versailles because it was ensconced there.] But the revolution was made.

Later, Lecomte and another General, Clément Thomas, were taken prisoner before being shot. This incident would become the centre of controversy for years to come, trotted out by enemies of the Communards to demonstrate their barbarism. Of course, the two men's role in perpetrating mass violence to crush the revolution of 1848 and Lecomte's repeated orders to kill women and children are rarely mentioned.

Hostile witnesses viewed events through the jaundiced eyes of those accustomed to wielding unchallenged authority, but the narrative is the same. A Versailles army officer recorded that where he was in charge they were stopped by a crowd of several hundred local inhabitants, principally children and women. The infantry detachment which was there to escort the cannon completely forgot their duty and dispersed into the crowd, succumbing to its perfidious seductions, and ending by turning up their rifle butts.

A proclamation by Thiers was posted around the city: the taking of the cannon was "indispensable to the maintenance of order", the intention of the government was to rid the city of the "insurrectionary committee" propagating "communist" doctrines, threatening Paris with pillage. This slur that the rebels wanted to destroy Paris, issued by the reactionary who had abandoned Paris to be shelled and occupied by the Prussians, was the source of even more determined resistance.

Once the horses arrived, some soldiers succeeded in beginning to move some of the cannon in Belleville. Guardsmen and residents responded by building barricades to physically prevent their removal. The crowd swelled, transforming itself from a mass of spectators to increasingly angry and active participants. One observer wrote that they saw:

> women and children swarming up the hillside in a compact mass; the artillery tried in vain to fight their way through the crowd, but the waves of people engulfed everything, surging over the cannon-mounts, over the ammunition wagons, under the wheels, under the horses' feet, paralysing the advance of the riders who spurred on their mounts in vain. The horses reared and lunged forward, their sudden movement clearing the crowd, but the space was filled at once by a back-wash created by the surging multitude.

In response to a call by a National Guardsman, women cut through the horses' harnesses. The soldiers began dismounting, accepting the offers of food and wine from the women. As they broke ranks they became "the object of frenetic ovations".

Some time later the *Times* correspondent returned to Montmartre and visited the barricade, the first stone of which he had seen laid. It had now

> grown to considerable dimensions by reason of the rule which is enforced that every passer must place a stone, a pile of which is placed for the purpose on each side of the street... New barricades were springing up in every direction... It was now midday, and the whole affair wore a most strange and incomprehensible aspect to one not brought up to making barricades... Instead of a government blocking every street as was the case in the morning, a hostile cannon was now looking down every street.

The barricades would develop their own centres of activity, drama and tragedy which would become a focus for historians. Eric Hazan, in his book *The Invention of Paris, a History in Footsteps*, includes a history of barricades and their "theatrical role" with reference to the Commune's use of them.

Cordons of soldiers had been replaced by National Guards supervising barricade-building. The streets, so quiet first thing in the morning, were now "swarming with [Guardsmen], drums were beating, bugles blowing, and all the din of victory".

By midday, General Vinoy, assigned to capture the cannon, was fleeing Paris. A Commune sympathizer wrote in his diary:

> Legally we had no more government; no police force or policemen; no magistrate or trials; no top officials or prefects; the landlords had run away in a panic abandoning their build-

ings to the tenants, no soldiers or generals; no letters or telegrams; no customs officials, tax collectors or teachers. No more Academy or Institute: the great professors, doctors and surgeons had left... Paris, immense Paris was abandoned to the "orgies of the vile multitude.

How to explain this seemingly spontaneous mass mobilization over a few hundred cannon? Paris had been under siege by the Prussians since 19 September 1870 and shelled relentlessly since 5 January. Anger with Thiers was intense. He had gone to war with Germany the previous July for the glory of the French empire. Confronted with defeat by Bismarck's army, he baulked at the idea of arming the population of Paris. And the bourgeoisie refused to support any defence of Paris while the National Guard, with its working-class membership, remained in control of armaments. It was clear that to win the war with Bismarck, all cities, especially Paris, needed to be mobilized under arms. But the history of France since the revolution of 1789 had been one of recurring social upheavals which terrified the bourgeoisie. An army general later summed up the problem: "the diplomacy of the government and almost all of the defence revolved around one thing: *the fear of revolt*". So Thiers had conspired with Prussia's Bismarck to crush radical Paris as a condition of a treaty to end the war. Removing the cannon was part of that process.

"Paris armed is the revolution armed", remarks Marx. And so Thiers, "by surrendering to Prussia not only Paris, but all France...initiated the civil war they were now to wage, with the assistance of Prussia, against the republic and Paris".

Attempting to seize the cannon was in reality simply the trigger which unleashed a well of bitterness fed by poverty and squalor in the overcrowded working-class districts. The restructuring of Paris

by Georges-Eugène Haussmann, [Usually known as Baron Hauss-
mann] appointed by Louis Napoléon Bonaparte, who ruled from
his coup d'état in 1852 until September 1870, had been devastating.
New, wide boulevards cut swathes through workers' districts, destroying 100,000 apartments in 20,000 buildings. This displaced
thousands from central Paris, with the poor crowding into Montmartre and Belleville.

In the midst of a booming economy, it is estimated that a majority of the working class required government assistance. Alongside
growing misery, the wealthy enjoyed glitzy arcades packed with el-
egant stores and cafés within walking distance of their magnificent
private residences. As Merriman says, "the bourgeoisie's day had
truly arrived". The rebuilding of Paris, which was meant to stave off
social unrest, had instead stoked it for decades.

The victorious movement of March 1871 had brought to life
what became known as the Paris Commune. Its task was now to reorganize life in the city, based on principles of justice, equality and
freedom from tyranny.

The Commune – a new power

As we follow events over the next 72 days we will witness truly awe-
inspiring achievements. Innovative democratic institutions were established. And the experience of taking control over their society
inspired mass involvement in debates about all aspects of their lives.
They replaced the state with one under their control. They vig-
orously attempted radical reforms in the family, the conditions of
women, in the workplace, and education, well ahead of the times, as
they debated the role of science, religion and the arts in society.

Edmond de Goncourt – co-founder of the naturalist school of literature in France and whose will established the Goncourt Academy which annually awards the prestigious French literary prize – left this testimony to the Commune's proletarian character:

> The triumphant revolution seems to be taking possession of Paris...barricades are being put up everywhere, naughty children scramble on top of them... You are overcome with disgust to see their stupid and abject faces, which triumph and drunkenness have imbued with a kind of radiant swinishness...for the moment France and Paris are under the control of workmen... How long will it last?... The unbelievable rules...the cohorts of Belleville throng our conquered boulevard.

He is disgusted by their "mocking astonishment" at their achievement, noting that they wear their shoes without socks! He admits that the "government is leaving the hands of those who have, to go into the hands of those who have not".

By midday on 18 March, the population had established a situation of dual power: radical Paris in a standoff with the government in Versailles.

On one side was Adolph Theirs, a reactionary through and through. His government, elected as recently as February, had already fled to the decadent safety of Versailles, accompanied by the army and a stream of bourgeois and respectable middle-class figures. Now it operated from the Grand Château of the Bourbon monarchy in Versailles, the reactionary centre of the centuries-old alliance between the Catholic church and the Bourbons. Thiers, determined to crush the Commune, would be backed by all of respectable opinion, both in France and across Europe.

On the other side of the barricades, workers created the most democratic institutions known to humanity at that time. Marx would write of their achievements: "[t]he great social measure of the Commune was its own working existence. Its special measures could but betoken the tendency of a government of the people by the people". Such a state of affairs was a direct threat to the repressive rule of Thiers, the monarchy and the church.

Whenever the oppressed rise up and fight for their rights, a sense of revelry inevitably follows. This is what inspires sympathetic witnesses of revolutions to describe such moments as festivals of the oppressed. Paris in 1871 was no different. Even bitter enemies of the Commune could not but convey the joyous atmosphere in the wake of the victory of 18 March. One recorded the experience of standing in front of the Hôtel de Ville, the Paris town hall now occupied by the Communards, while the names of those elected to form a Commune Committee were read out:

> I write these lines still full of emotion... One hundred thousand perhaps, where did they come from? From every corner of the city. Armed men spilled out of every nearby street, and the sharp points of the bayonets, glittering in the sun, made the place seem like a field of lightning. The music playing was *La Marseillaise*, a song taken up in fifty thousand resolute voices: this thunder shook all the people, and the great song, out of fashion from defeats, recovered for a moment its former energy...An immense sea of banners, bayonets, and caps, surging forward, drifting back, undulating, breaking against the stage. The cannons still thundered, but they were heard only in intervals between the singing. Then all the sounds merged into a single cheer, the universal voice of the countless

multitude, and all these people had but one heart just as they had but one voice.

The elected Commune Committee was entrusted with the momentous responsibility of defending the city against Versailles, organising food supplies, care for the wounded; indeed, of reorganising the entire life of the city.

The state

The old state power had been demolished, a move Marx emphasized:

> [F]or the first time since the days of February 1848, the streets of Paris were safe, and that without any police of any kind. "We," said a member of the Commune, "hear no longer of assassination, theft, and personal assault; it seems indeed as if the police had dragged along with it to Versailles all its Conservative friends".

To emphasize the significance of this, Marx puts it in a broader context:

> The direct antithesis to the empire was the Commune. The cry of "social republic" [the popular slogan of the mass movement]…did but express a vague aspiration after a republic that was not only to supersede the monarchical *form* of class rule, but class rule itself. The Commune was the positive form of that republic. Paris, the central seat of the old governmental power, and, at the same time, the social stronghold of the French working class, had risen in arms against the attempt

of Thiers...to restore and perpetuate that old governmental power bequeathed to them by the empire. Paris could resist only because, in consequence of the siege, it had got rid of the army, and replaced it by a National Guard, the bulk of which consisted of working men. This fact was now to be transformed into an institution. The first decree of the Commune, therefore, was the suppression of the standing army, and the substitution for it of the armed people.

This revolutionary move was the basis on which the new democracy that Marx celebrates could be built.

The majority of [the Commune Committee's] members were naturally working men, or acknowledged representatives of the working class. The Commune was to be a working, not a parliamentary body, executive and legislative at the same time. The Commune was formed of the municipal councillors, chosen by universal suffrage in the various wards of the town, responsible and revocable at short terms.

This was a key point Marx emphasized: how elected delegates and government officials can be made accountable. But not just elected delegates. "Like the rest of public servants, magistrates and judges were to be elective, responsible, and revocable."

Work

Marx concluded that these innovative democratic structures were "the political form at last discovered under which to work out the economical emancipation of labour" and explained:

The political rule of the producer cannot co-exist with the perpetuation of his social slavery. The Commune was therefore to serve as a lever for uprooting the economical foundation upon which rests the existence of classes, and therefore of class rule. With labour emancipated...productive labour ceases to be a class attribute.

The Commune Committee was not just left to get on with decreeing reforms while everything went back to the old normal. Historians have documented the incredible flowering of organization, debate and social experimentation that took place, adding a tapestry of rich detail which illuminates Marx's theoretical generalizations.

Many of the organizations and their proposals were based on demands which had been discussed by socialists and worker militants for decades. The difference now was that they were not just topics for debate and protest. Now they became the expression of the poor and oppressed as they began to take control of their lives.

The Committee set up a range of Commissions to deal with specific areas. The Jewish-Hungarian worker, Léo Frankel, a member of the International and collaborator of Marx, was appointed minister of labour to deal with workers' rights and working conditions.

Night work by bakers was abolished; employers were banned from reducing wages by levying their employees with fines under any pretext, "a process in which the employer combines in his own person the parts of legislator, judge, and executor, and filches the money to boot".

Some issues were complicated due to conflicting priorities. Military supplies were obviously of paramount importance. But the Commune's purchase of the cheapest equipment did not sit easily beside workers' demands for decent wages. The commissioner for finance, Proudhonist François Jourde, baulked at rewriting contracts with employers, hardly surprising given the Proudhonists supported private property. But as Frankel pointed out, "the revolution was made exclusively by the working class. I don't see what the point of the Commune is if we...do nothing for that class". In response to the workers themselves, new contracts specifying a satisfactory minimum wage were agreed. The employers were not consulted.

An additional clause decreed by the Labour Commission stated that where possible contracts be awarded "directly to the workers' own corporations". Workers' corporations can be understood here to refer to co-operatives, associations and trade unions. They were strongly backed by Frankel's Commission as a vehicle for socialism. The Commission also decreed that the enterprises of any employers who fled to Versailles were to be taken over by its workers.

Another of Marx's collaborators in the International played a key role in influencing the Labour Commission.[1] The Russian socialist Elisabeth Dmitrieff was central to establishing the *Union des Femmes*, or Women's Union. It was the women's section of the First International. A *mariage blanc*[2] had provided Dmitrieff with an escape route out of Russia. She had spent the last three months in London, where she met with Marx almost daily, discussing theories of revolution. Prior to that she had joined the International in Geneva, where she had met the future Communards Eugène Varlin and Benoît Malon. According to historian Kristin Ross, the *Union des Femmes* became the largest and most effective organization in the Commune. It met daily in almost every one of the twenty arrondissements. The membership was dominated by workers in the garment trades: seamstresses, laundresses, dressmakers and so on.

The *Union des Femmes*' discussions included theoretical questions about ending private property and the issues of gender-based inequality, as well as solving the day to day struggle to provide fuel and food to families. At the same time they participated in the defence of the Commune, maintenance of barricades, tending to the sick and wounded. Ross sums up: "In some ways, the Women's Union can be seen as the practical response to many of the questions and problems regarding women's labour that had been the discussion topic [for years]".

Another historian, Donny Gluckstein, argues: "[t]he Labour Commission's work was shaped by, and depended absolutely on, the Women's Union and the trade unions' workers' corporations, which in turn were empowered by the commission." Spelling out their mission, the *Union des Femmes* declared: "We want work, but in order to keep the product. No more exploiters, no more masters. Work and well-being for all". At their urging, the Commune set up cooperatives to make Guardsmen's uniforms, which provided well-paid work under the women workers' control.

While women suffered special oppression, their working lives were also shaped by the broader conditions facing the working class. They made remarkable moves in the direction towards workers' control, in spite of limited time and conditions of war: "There were a dozen confiscated workshops, above all those linked to military defence... Five corporations had begun searching out the available workshops, ready for their confiscation". And state-owned establishments such as the mint and the national print shop were put under workers' management. Even the café workers, given these leads, began to set up a trade union.

The radical clubs

The tradition of radical political clubs, inspired by the 1789–92 revolution and revived in 1848, had emerged from the underground in the year leading up to the Commune. They discussed a wide range of issues: political strategy, which reforms to prioritize, women's rights, attitudes to the church and science, how to better organize defence and strengthen the barricades and more. Previously these issues were confined to radical circles, but now the clubs attracted a wider audience and enthusiastic support for their proposals. Workers were the great majority of participants, but middle-class radicals also joined in. Between 36 and 50 clubs met daily, mostly in the working-class districts. Some were huge, involving thousands, with women playing a prominent role both in their own clubs and in mixed ones with men. Many discussions resulted in sending resolutions to the Commune Committee, and there was an ongoing debate regarding its relationship to the clubs.

An anti-Communard gave a sense of the spirit which made the clubs such a vibrant part of the new democracy:

> From Rue Druout right up to the Montmartre district the boulevards had become a permanent public meeting or club where the crowd, divided into groups, had filled not only the pavements but also the road to the point of blocking...traffic. They formed a myriad of public assemblies where war and peace were hotly debated.

Élie Reclus, an ethnographer given responsibility for the management and preservation of the Bibliothèque Nationale, called them "schools for the people", where constructive debate flourished and a heightened sense of community was created. Ross describes the clubs as "a quasi-Brechtian merging of pedagogy and entertainment".

A week after the declaration of the elected Commune Committee, on the initiative of the club in the third arrondissement that was endorsed by the Commune Committee, churches across the city were commandeered as meeting places and organising centres. These venues, unlike street meetings, created a sense of seriousness and permanence in the clubs, even of high drama.

Lissagaray, member of the International and author of one of the first books published about the Commune, penned a colourful description of one such meeting:

> The Revolution mounts the pulpits...almost hidden by the shadow of the vaults, hangs the figure of Christ draped in the popular oriflamme. The only luminous centre is the reading desk, facing the pulpit, hung with red. The organ and the people chant *La Marseillaise.* The orator, over-excited by these fantastic surroundings, launches forth into ecstatic declamations which the echo repeats like a menace. The people discuss the events of the day, the means of defence; the members of the Commune are severely censured, and vigorous resolutions are voted to be presented to the Hôtel de Ville the next day.[3]

It is wonderful to imagine such revolutionary proceedings taking place beneath soaring ceilings and beautiful stained glass windows. Occupying these odes to privilege and power was a constant reminder of the momentous challenge the Commune had thrown down before the bourgeoisie, the monarchy and their ally, the church.

Separating church and state

Marx noted that once the state force was dismantled, the Commune:

was anxious to break the spiritual force of repression...by the disestablishment and disendowment of all churches as proprietary bodies... The whole of the educational institutions were opened to the people gratuitously, and at the same time cleared of all interference of church and state. Thus, not only was education made accessible to all, but science itself freed from the fetters which class prejudice and governmental force had imposed upon it.

Anti-church sentiment was not just the preserve of small numbers of radicals. The Catholic church had thrown its wealth and power behind Bonaparte's dictatorship, never concealing its bitter hostility to republicanism. So the growing opposition to Bonaparte was organically anti-clerical, among both middle-class radicals and the urban poor.

In the large cities, attendance at religious ceremonies had sharply declined before the revolution, especially among workers. It's not difficult to see why. The church taught that the poor would be rewarded for their suffering by passing from this vale of tears to the glories of heaven. But to enter that heaven you had to silently endure endless misery.

As well, the church, in this time of the Enlightenment and a rapidly changing world, was seen as a bastion of ignorance, summed up by the *Syllabus of Errors* in 1864 which denounced modern society. As Merriman writes: "[t]he church's close association with people of means had long drawn popular ire; the birth of the Commune merely unleashed it".

State laws were strongly influenced by the church's teachings about the family, women's role and morality. So the programs for reforms raised in the clubs around such issues were more often than not entwined with anti-religious bitterness.

There were no bounds to the irreverence displayed once the churches were commandeered. Mock masses, holy water replaced with a pile of tobacco, statues of the Virgin Mary dressed in the uniform of women supplying provisions to the National Guard, sometimes with a pipe in her mouth. At the same time the Communards in many cases allowed ceremonies for the devout to go ahead in the mornings before the clubs met. As such the meetings would often take place amidst flowers, crucifixes and other religious paraphernalia left behind from morning mass and other religious events.

Church properties provided much needed venues, a practical issue which just happened to intersect with the anti-church sentiment. Notre-Dame-de-Lorette became a barracks at one stage, then a jail for those arrested for refusing to fight. The Women's Union's cooperative was housed in Saint-Pierre in Montmartre, also used as a storage place for munitions and a school for girls. Another became a medical facility. In a reversal of the old order, speakers in the clubs insisted that the clergy pay rent to the Commune for use of ecclesiastical spaces for "their comedies". Proceeds were to go to the widows and orphans of the fighting. The club of Faubourg Saint-Antoine suggested that church bells be melted to make cannon.

The hostility to the church is a theme in many records of the time. For instance, when the archbishop, who had been arrested, called the head of police and court officials "my children", the sharp response was: "We are not children – we are the magistrates of the people!" Merriman cites a document in which the archbishop is described as "Prisoner A who says he is a servant of somebody called God".

While one third of all students attended religious schools, the church exercised a virtual monopoly over the education of girls, a fact directly related to the lower rates of literacy among women. In general, religious education was backward and stifling. A commission headed by a range of artists, teachers and songwriters instigated closing down the church schools and removing religious symbols. Where necessary, crowds took direct action to shut schools taught by religious figures, who had never been required to have the qualifications demanded of regular teachers. Many of them resigned, asking for lay teachers to replace them. By May religious teaching was banned in all schools.

Education

Members of the First International were prominent in debating and proposing innovations on a number of intersecting questions around education. The official journal of the Commune records that they were active in organising public educational meetings and reorganising education "on the largest of possible bases". Ross puts well how central was the issue:

> A lived experience of "equality in action", the Commune was primarily a set of dismantling acts directed at the state bureaucracy and performed by ordinary men and women. Many of these dismantling acts were focused, not surprisingly, on that central bureaucracy: the schools.

Discussions about education went well beyond secularization. A third of children had no access to education at all, and the Commune would try to implement compulsory and equal education for both boys and girls. Teachers' wages were raised, with women and men on equal pay. A school of industrial arts was established with a woman as director. Students would receive scientific and literary instruction, then use some of the day for the application of art and drawing to industry. One of the most enthusiastic supporters of the polytechnic schools was Eugène Pottier, member of the International and a supporter of the utopian socialist Charles Fourier's concept of "attractive work". A son of a box-maker, Pottier was a fabric designer and a poet.

Unlike today, theoretical and practical debates about education were not carried out in the rarefied circles of academia, but in the clubs around the city. Declarations reflecting those debates were printed as posters and pasted on walls in the streets. One which bore Pottier's name read in part:

> That each child of either sex, having completed the cycle of primary studies, may leave school possessing the serious elements of one or two manual professions: this is our goal...the last word in human progress is entirely summed up by the simple phrase: *Work by everyone, for everyone*

"Secular nurseries" were also set up near workplaces employing women. They were guided by principles laid down by the utopian socialist Charles Fourier: caregivers were not to wear black or dark-coloured clothing, and were rotated to avoid boredom or tiredness setting in, "it being important that children should be looked after only by cheerful and young women, whenever possible".

Religious representations were replaced with pictures and sculptures of real objects such as animals and trees, including aviaries full of birds. Boredom was thought to be "the greatest malady" of children. We get a glimpse of some of what those children were taught in this anecdote from a gentleman who witnessed a "band" of 200 "toddlers" marching behind a drum and a small red flag. "They sing at the top of their lungs *La Marseillaise*. This grotesque parade celebrated the opening of a lay school organized by the Commune."

Marx's collaborator, Benoît Malon, helped set up an asylum for orphans and runaways, where they could be offered basic instruction. Paule Mincke opened one of the first schools for girls. They requisitioned a Jesuit school, because it was endowed with the most advanced equipment and laboratories.

Édouard Vaillant set up a professional school of industrial art for girls, occupying the École des Beaux Arts. This school introduced a new approach to teaching. Any skilled worker over the age of 40 could apply to become a professor.

The emphasis on science as fundamental to the advance of society was a powerful theme. A young scientist from the US, Mary Putnam Jacobi, happened to be in Paris. Her experience in that spring "led to a political awakening" and inspired her to spend the next three decades campaigning against sexist assumptions about women's biology.

She became a powerful advocate for the equal contribution of women to medicine and developed the philosophy that the advance of science and the advance of women were one and the same objective. She depathologized menstruation by disproving the then widely held notion that rest was necessary in order to prevent infertility, one of the reactionary ideas of the Proudhonists.

Women's rights and the family

Marx mocks "the absconding men of family, religion, and, above all, of property", and writes:

> In their stead, the real women of Paris showed again at the surface – heroic, noble, and devoted, like the women of antiquity. Working, thinking, fighting, bleeding Paris – almost

forgetful, in its incubation of a new society, of the Cannibals at its gates – radiant in the enthusiasm of its historic initiative!

As already discussed, women were involved in pushing many of the Commune's most radical proposals. This is not surprising. Women – due to the specific nature of their oppression – can be the bearers of more conservative ideas in stable times, especially when trapped in the home. But when they challenge their chains of oppression, they often become the most dynamic element of mass movements, with less to lose and more to gain from a fundamental transformation of the status quo.

The Commune immediately made farsighted and fundamental improvements to women's lives. The remission of rents and the ban on sales of goods deposited at the pawn shops lifted a huge burden from workers' families. A decree on 10 April granted wives – legal or de facto – of Guardsmen who were killed defending the Commune a pension of 600 francs. Each of her children, legitimate or not, could collect 365 francs until they turned 18. And orphans would receive the education necessary "to make their own way in society".

As Edith Thomas, in her social history of women in the Commune, remarks: "This was an implicit recognition of the structure of the working-class family, as it really existed, outside the context of religious and bourgeois laws". *Unions libres* were common among workers but not recognized by the church or the state, denying women their dignity, to say nothing of economic discrimination given that unmarried women were not eligible for any widow's allowance. And "[i]n a city where about a quarter of all couples were unmarried, the church, which normally charged 2 francs to register a birth, demanded 7.50 francs [about two days' wages for many] for an 'illegitimate' child".

Thomas comments that the widows' pension was "one of the most revolutionary steps of its brief reign. That this measure outraged the bourgeoisie, and that it was received with jubilation by members of the Commune are indications of its significance".

But women weren't passive recipients of reforms. It was mostly women who dragged the guillotine into Rue Voltaire and burned it on 10 April. Women were some of the most militant in both women's and mixed clubs. They were particularly strident in their denunciation of marriage. In a club in Les Halles, a militant woman warned that marriage "is the greatest error of ancient humanity. To be married is to be a slave. In the club of Saint-Ambroise a woman declared that she would not permit her sixteen-year-old daughter to marry, that she was perfectly happy living with a man "without the blessing of the Church". At least one other club also voted in favour of divorce, a policy which was implemented by the Commune Committee.

These kinds of discussions in the clubs were the catalyst for the kinds of reforms we have seen. They didn't just come from the Commune Committee on high. And marriage ceased to be a formal contract, it was simply a written agreement between couples, easily dissolved.

Michel's *Club de la Révolution*, along with others, raised the right to abortion, which was endorsed by the Committee. At the Club of the Free Thinkers Nathalie Lemel – a book binder, and member of Marx's group in the International who worked with that other comrade of Marx, Elisabeth Dmitrieff and her *Union des Femmes* – along with Lodoyska Kawecka, who dressed in trousers and wore two revolvers hanging from her sash, argued for divorce and the liberation of women.

Many of the ideas about women's liberation, just as those about education, did not originate in the Commune. Marx's grouping in the International, along with feminists such as André Léo, had created a tradition of support for these attitudes among the most militant workers and socialists. But the revolutionary movement opened up a whole new opportunity for their ideas to win popular support.

The role of art

The anti-capitalist, anti-elitist orientation of the International naturally attracted artists, writers and other intelligentsia whose dependence on patronage and state subsidies curtailed their artistic and political expression.

Eugène Pottier has become famous for his authorship of *The Internationale,* a song imbued with all the internationalism and irreverence of the Commune. Before that he also wrote the founding manifesto of the Artists' Federation in which he penned the term "Communal luxury", adopted by Kristin Ross as the title of her book.

The founder and president of the Federation was Gustave Courbet, later persecuted because he was accused of ordering the demolition of the Vendôme column. The Federation held debates about the role of art and the artist in society, the integration of art into everyday life and how to overcome the counterposition between beauty and utility. It attracted well-known artists such as Corot, Manet and Daumier, who scorned those who fled Paris for Versailles such as Cézanne, Pissarro and Degas. Émile Zola, who associated with the reactionaries in Versailles, disgraced himself with mocking attacks on Courbet for his participation in politics, a sphere considered foreign to artists.

The Federation refused to deal with any artistic creations which were not signed by their creator. This was a response to the previous practice of artists having to sell their works unsigned so that a dealer could pocket the profits. The personal history of Napoléon Gaillard, another member of the International, demonstrates their theories. A shoemaker, Gaillard was appointed commissioner for barricades. But how to sign a creation as immense as a barricade? An enemy of the Commune explained how Gaillard solved this problem:

> [He] appeared so proud of his creation that on the morning of May 20, we saw him in full commandant's uniform, four gold braids on the sleeve and cap, red lapels on his tunic, great riding boots, long, flowing hair, a steady gaze...and with his hand on his hip, had himself photographed.

In harmony with the theories developed in the Federation, Gaillard would write philosophical treatises on the foot and the boot, and invent rubber galoshes. There were people who would not wear any other shoe than those he designed, years after his death. From exile he wrote "[t]he Art of the Shoe is, no matter what one says, of all the arts the most difficult, the most useful, and above all the least understood". He insisted that he be known as both a worker and an "artist shoemaker".

His stance and writings summed up the Artists' Federation's arguments for overcoming the counterposition of the useful to the beautiful, calling for the public to demand shoes made for the foot as it is, rather than as it is assumed it should be.

The attempt to overcome the separation of art from industry and life in general became a subject of much debate and experimentation, strongly influencing the British socialist novelist and fabric designer William Morris.

The Commune's internationalism

Marx and Engels had argued in *The German Ideology* decades earlier that workers could only become fit to create a new society through struggle against the old. Paris in March 1871 illustrated their point dramatically. France had been at war with Prussia since July 1870, yet the Commune was determinedly internationalist in spirit: "Within sight of that Prussian army, that had annexed to Germany two French provinces, the Commune annexed to France the working people all over the world". A Jewish-Hungarian worker was appointed to the key position of minister of labour. They "honoured the heroic sons of Poland [J Dabrowski and W Wróblewski] by placing them at the head of the defenders of Paris". And "to broadly mark the new era of history it was conscious of initiating, under the eyes of the conquering Prussians on one side, and the Bonapartist army...on the other, the Commune pulled down that colossal symbol of martial glory, the Vendôme Column".

This was not just a militant, spur of the moment act. Great thought and planning went into the removal of the statue that was on top of the column. There is a photograph of a pile of rubble in the Place Vendôme, all that remains of Bonaparte's statue, surrounded by undamaged buildings: the Communards had employed their most skilled engineers and workers to bring it down. Indeed, their original goal was to move the monument to a museum, but it proved too fragile to survive the toppling. The Place Vendôme was renamed Place Internationale.

Like many of the reforms being proposed, the ideas of internationalism had been developing among radical workers before March 1871. Lissagaray outlines the development of a combative working class, independent of the increasingly conservative liberal bourgeoisie. In 1870, as rumours circulated about war with Prussia:

> [T]he revolutionary socialists crowd the boulevards crying, *Vive la paix!* And singing the pacific refrain – "The people are our brothers/And the tyrants are our enemies"... Unable to influence the bourgeoisie, they turn to the working men of Germany... "Brothers, we protest against the war, we who wish for peace, labour and liberty. Brothers, do not listen to the hirelings who seek to deceive you as to the real wishes of France".

The Commune's embrace of foreign militants in their midst and the demolition of the symbol of imperial might demonstrated that their internationalism was more than rhetorical.

Reorganising society democratically

Contemporary observers, both hostile and sympathetic, commented that the Commune's elected leaders were unknown. That was not as true as it might seem; many of them had already made their name in debates in the popular clubs. To respectable society, then as now, such mass leaders were invisible. The other comment which recurs throughout the observations then and through all the histories is their inexperience. And how could it be otherwise? As Marx stresses, this was the first time workers had been sufficiently formed as a class to lead a movement for change. So even experienced activists were tackling new questions.

Donny Gluckstein looks at the way the democracy worked in some detail. He correctly puts it in the context of having to defend the Commune against Versailles with its trained army against the much smaller numbers of the rag-tag forces of the National Guard.

Prisoners of war were released by Bismarck to help crush Paris. They were bombarded with lies and horror stories about the intentions of the Parisians, whipped into a frenzy of hatred that would be unleashed in the last week of May. But that murderous final stanza was merely the conclusion of growing bombardments and incursions into Paris by the army. These attacks killed scores of Guardsmen, with many others arrested.

Given these conditions, the humanitarian principles the Commune sought to live by often conflicted with the need for defence. For instance, the abolition of the death penalty distanced the idea of revolution from such cruelty. But in the face of massacres and hostages disappearing into the Versailles jails, it was reinstated. Only three were ever executed, but as we subsequently saw following the October Revolution in Russia, there is an unavoidable tension between honourable long-term goals and the immediate question of survival.

Gluckstein shows how the Commune Committee – headquartered in the Hôtel de Ville – related to the network of committees in the arrondissements, the clubs, and myriad other organizations which flourished. He argues that "the main living link between the mass movement and the Communal Council was the clubs".

We cannot understand how democracy functioned in the Commune without grasping the vibrant life of those clubs. They argued for the creation of a stronger leadership in the form of a Committee of Public Safety, which provoked widespread debates. The name invoked the terror of the Great Revolution, which contradicted the image of remaining lawful and pacific which the leaders at the Hôtel de Ville had insisted on. Some women formed their own vigilance committees in spite of reluctance from the Commune Committee. The club Saint-Séverin, possibly where supporters of the International had some sway, asked the Commune to "finish off the bourgeoisie in one blow [and] take over the Banque de France", a point Marx had made on multiple occasions.

A meeting of 3,000 at Louise Michel's *Club de la Révolution* on 13 May, just a week before the final bloody week, unanimously called for the abolition of magistrates, the immediate arrest of priests and the execution of a hostage every 24 hours until the release of political prisoners by Versailles. These are the demands of some of the most radical Communards, which shows both the level of debate and how arguments made by organized militants could get a mass audience. This was partly helped by the indecision in the Hôtel de Ville, which inflamed popular impatience.

Clubs insisted they should oversee the actions of the Commune Committee. Eleven of them formed a federation to produce a bulletin, some summoned the Council members to attend their meetings so there was more of an exchange of views. These chaotic events reflected both the dynamism which had been unleashed, but also much confusion about how to win against the increasingly threatening Versailles troops. Gluckstein concludes that it was the "sections" which included organizations such as the *Union des Femmes* that most effectively worked with the Hôtel de Ville, establishing a "strong and reciprocal" relationship: "In education, for example, much of the momentum came not from the Commune's commission but from the pre-existing bodies of educators". And we have already seen the reciprocal role of the *Union des Femmes* in relation to the Commission of Labour and the Commune Committee.

This issue of how the clubs pressured the Commune Committee, took initiatives and demanded that the Committee inform them of their decisions is important in understanding the role of women in the revolutionary process. Judy Cox correctly challenges Gay Gullickson who, like most historians, downplays the advances for women because they weren't members of the elected Commune

Committee. This is doubly mistaken. Firstly, like many feminists, Gullickson assumes that men can't represent women's interests. But support for women's rights is not simply a question of gender, but of politics. As Cox points out, "The Marxist wing of the First International was the only political organization in France which supported the female franchise. At least four socialist male members of the Commune – Eugène Varlin, Benoît Malon, Édouard Vaillant and Leó Frankel – took initiatives that promoted women's equality in their areas of responsibility".

But it was not simply a matter of principled men standing up against oppression. As already indicated, women's voices were loud and clear in the clubs, on the barricades and in every activity of the Commune. To modern supporters of women's liberation, the fact that women weren't granted the right to vote in the elections seems shocking. But there is no evidence that women demanded it. As Ross says:

> The [Women's] Union showed no trace of interest in parliamentary or rights-based demands. In this its members were, like Louise Michel, Paule Mincke and other women in the Commune, indifferent to the vote (a major goal in 1848) and to traditional forms of republican politics... Participation in public life, in other words, was for them in no way tied to the franchise.

This is true, but the National Committee of the New Guard assumed, when they found themselves at the head of a successful insurrection, that they should operate legally. So the elections for which they got agreement from the mayors were held under the government's existing law, which only allowed for male suffrage. We don't know what the outcome would have been if prominent women had led a fight for female suffrage, but it is clear that many would have backed them.

Gullickson takes the positions of the right-wing Proudhonists – against whom Marx campaigned relentlessly – as evidence of a general chauvinist male culture which sidelined women. But even the left of the Proudhonists, such as Lefrançais, supported women's rights. And in spite of her feminism, Gullickson does not respect the voice of André Léo, a prominent feminist from well before the Commune and editor of the magazine *La Sociale*. [This was the pseudonym of Victoire Léodile Béra, under which she wrote several novels, and the name she is known by in the records of the Commune.]

To bolster her case Gullickson quotes an account Léo published of New Guard officers and a physician who acted disrespectfully towards women volunteers. Yet Léo concluded that very article with: "we noticed the very different attitudes present. Without exception the [middle-class] officers and surgeons showed a lack of sympathy that varied from coldness to insults; but from the National Guards came respect and fraternity". And, because she aired the grievance against the officers, Louis Rossel, the Commune's war delegate, asked her for advice about involving more women in the military campaign.

Of course not everyone was immediately convinced of the most radical points described here. The point is that women were challenging backward views, agitating for the reforms they needed, and the Commune endorsed their demands. The majority of Léo's articles in *La Sociale* dealt with issues not specifically about women. But when she did, she emphasized the need *and the potential* for solidarity between the sexes. One of her articles was titled "*Toutes avec Tous*" (all women and men together).

We can add a further point. Gullickson can't recognize the immense advances that women made, and the tradition they left for the working class to learn from because she, like other liberal feminists, focuses on elected leaders. While what happens at that level is not irrelevant, socialists should focus on the changes taking place below the surface, where workers were busy establishing democratic structures, raising new ideas and taking incredible initiatives. In the tumultuous events that characterize any revolution, the democratic character of the process cannot be fully understood simply by analysing constitutions or formal structures. It is about the dynamic of that process, and the incipient tendencies that emerge spontaneously through the struggle which can be developed further by conscious political intervention.

Much of the retrospective critiques of the Commune identify their failure to seize the wealth stored in the National Bank as a key mistake. Yet this itself was partly a product of the rigorous democracy that was the norm throughout the Commune. Raoul Rigault, a Blanquist and member of the International, was in charge of the "ex-Prefecture of police". He was a colourful figure with a history of political agitation and organising, dubbed the "professor of barricades" by a magistrate in one of his many trials. He ordered some guards to seize the Bank of France to nationalise the wealth stored there. But prone to the elitism typical of the Blanquists, he did not consult with the rest of the Communal Council, and so the proposal was blocked by the Proudhonists. One of them insisted that the bank "should be respected as private property belonging to the shareholders"! By the time the Communal Council considered Rigault's instruction, the opportunity had been missed.

Engels maintained that "[t]he bank in the hands of the Commune – this would have been worth more than 10,000 hostages". It is debatable whether this would have pushed Versailles to settle for peace as Engels asserted, but it is clear that the money within could have been used to deepen the Commune's achievements. For instance, the Commune had to spend 21 million francs on defence, leaving just 1,000 francs for education, an issue dear to the heart of virtually all who participated. More to the point, such reluctance to take on a bastion of governmental power and the bourgeoisie reflected the constant desire to operate within the bounds of bourgeois legality and to avoid being cast as responsible for the civil war raging around them. While there are examples of a lack of accountability from some leaders, the weaknesses historians identify have to be seen in the context of the siege, the civil war, and social and economic breakdown. The significant achievement is that which Marx emphasized: the embryo of a workers' democracy, with elected and recallable representatives, plus judges and officials at every level. This historical breakthrough warrants our main emphasis, rather than the understandable shortcomings.

A final point. The structures established by the Commune cannot be taken as a direct model for revolutionaries today. The working class in Paris was the largest group, numbering 900,000, surrounded by 400,000 petty bourgeois running 4,000 greengrocers' shops, 1,900 butchers, 1,300 bakeries. However, Haussmann's reconstruction of Paris had discouraged the establishment of large workplaces. Those that were established were mostly in the outer rim of Paris. The Cail plant in north-east Paris, employing 2,800 to produce steam engines and locomotives, was the exception rather than the norm. Workplaces of over 10 workers were only seven percent of the total, with 31 percent employing between two and ten. Gluckstein concludes:

> The nature of production...had an influence on the organizational structure of the 1871 movement... Trade union action was difficult to mount and broad activities could not easily be built from tiny workplaces. Such units of production could

not provide a collective focus for the working class. Instead that came from the National Guard and the clubs which offered a framework for collective expression and organization.

In the Russian revolution of 1905 workers would take another leap forward and create soviets, reflecting the huge growth of the industrial working class, brought together in workplaces massively larger than anything in Paris in 1871. This meant that the focus of organization shifted to the workplace, even as the streets remained an important focal point for large and united protests that brought workers from across different industries together. This is profoundly important.

As Rosa Luxemburg argued, "where the chains of oppression are forged, there they must be broken". Nevertheless the principles of the Commune lived on in the soviets: all delegates and people in places of responsibility to be recallable at any time, accountable to the electors, paid workers' wages and remaining at work where they experienced the conditions about which they made decisions. The Paris Commune is therefore best understood as a premonition, or a *harbinger*, of a future society. In Marx's words:

> The working class did not expect miracles from the Commune. They have no ready-made utopias to introduce *par décret du peuple*. They know that in order to work out their own emancipation...they will have to pass through long struggles, through a series of historic processes, transforming circumstances and men. They have no ideals to realize, but to set free the elements of the new society.

Some aspects of the Commune have been superseded by subsequent developments, and we do not know precisely how the working-class revolution of this century might look. However the basic principles of collectivity and democracy it established remain vitally important to the modern working class.

Ruling class savagery – *la semaine sanglante*

Marx had argued that we make our own history, but not in circumstances of our choosing. The uprising which erupted on 18 March forced the Communards to reorganize society amidst a Prussian siege and a bitter civil war. These factors strongly contributed to the defeat of this heroic uprising.

On Sunday 21 May, troops from Versailles stormed Paris. New barricades went up in street after street, as the population mobilized for a final heroic attempt to maintain their Commune. An eyewitness described how one of the barricades was constructed and defended by "a women's battalion of around a hundred and twenty. At the time that I arrived, a dark form detached itself from a carriage gate. It was a girl with a Phrygian bonnet over her ear, a musket in her hand, and a cartridge-belt at her waist. 'Halt, citizen, you don't pass here!'" We see how women have developed from pleading with soldiers not to shoot in March, to now playing a role as proud, fighting combatants in May, prepared to die with dignity and honour.

Just one week later, 30,000 or more people had been murdered by the counter-revolutionaries. The chapter headings used by Lissagaray in his book sum up the experience: "The Versailles fury", "The balance sheet of bourgeois vengeance". The essence of the events is captured in the title of John Merriman's book, *Massacre*. Though there are debates about the death toll, I see no point in quibbling about the precise figures. Many casualties were never recorded, their bodies thrown into mass graves and later incinerated.

Countless others disappeared into jails or colonial transportation, where who knows how many died. Others fled to seek sanctuary, and there are few records of who survived wounds inflicted in the fighting. This barbarity was at first cheered on in the respectable bourgeois papers of Europe, whose journalists had followed the army around "like jackals". One journalist had called for "an end to this international democratic vermin" of Red Paris. But faced with "the smell of carnage", swarms of flies on corpses, trees stripped of leaves, the streets full of dead birds, even some of these bourgeois commentators were repulsed. "Let us not kill any more", pleaded the *Paris Journal*, "Enough executions, enough blood, enough victims" lamented the *Nationale*.

But the upper classes who lived off the labour of those being massacred expressed no such limits to their savagery. Respectable women took tours of the dungeons where the arrested were incarcerated, holding their lace-edged handkerchiefs – made by the women at whom they gawked – to their noses against the stench of filth and dying Communards. In particular, they took delight in poking the women with their parasols. Many public figures, including judges and other respectable bourgeois and middle-class types, continued to bay for blood. To justify this frenzy, they invented lies which appealed to the prejudices of this scum. An anonymous Englishman described the Communards as "lashed up to a frenzy which has converted them into a set of wild beasts caught in a trap". This, in his opinion, "render[ed] their extermination a necessity". The ruling class especially hated the women Communards, whom they depicted as "vile", "wild" and sexually depraved.

Their fury was stoked by hysterical stories of the infamous *pétroleuses,* supposedly prepared to burn down the whole of Paris. So the legend of the *pétroleuses* demands our attention. Edith Thomas titled her book on the women of the Commune *Les Pétroleuses,* translated as *The Women Incendiaries*. She examines the evidence and concludes that it's not clear whether there were any *pétroleuses* in the way reactionaries used the term. At the same time, the Communards clearly did use fire as a weapon of war to destroy buildings from which the Versaillese could gun people down. Fire was also used as a form of barricade, a wall of flames to keep the soldiers back, set by the fighters who must have included women and possibly even children. Merriman documents orders given by the war delegate with the National Guard, Charles Delescluze, the ageing Jacobin, and others, including men in the Commune Committee, to blow up or set fire to houses.

Delescluze, aware that it had become impossible to muster the kind of military response necessary to repel the soldiers, "adopted a strategy of mass popular resistance". Generals of the National Guard specifically ordered "the burning of a number of monumental Parisian buildings, all in the fancy parts of town", as well as official buildings. One of the Communard generals ordered the Tuileries Palace to be set ablaze. Gustave Lefrançais, the most left-wing Proudhonist, admitted that he was one of those "who had shutters of joy seeing that sinister palace go up in flames".When a woman asked Nathalie Lemel what it was she could see burning in Montmartre, Lemel replied simply, "it's nothing at all, only the Palais-Royal and the Tuileries, because we do not want a king anymore".

Marx was right to defend the burning of the city:

> The working men's Paris, in the act of its heroic self-holo-caust, involved in its flames buildings and monuments. While tearing to pieces the living body of the proletariat, its rulers must no longer expect to return triumphantly into the intact architecture of their abodes. The government of Versailles cries, "Incendiarism!" and whispers this cue to all its

agents...to hunt up its enemies everywhere as suspect of pro-fessional incendiarism. The bourgeoisie of the whole world, which looks complacently upon the wholesale massacre after the battle, is convulsed by horror at the desecration of brick and mortar!

...The Commune used fire strictly as a means of defence. They used it to stop up to the Versailles troops those long, straight avenues which Haussmann had expressly opened to artillery-fire; they used it to cover their retreat, in the same way as the Versaillese, in their advance, used their shells which de-stroyed at least as many buildings as the fire of the Commune. It is a matter of dispute, even now, which buildings were set fire to by the defence, and which by the attack. And the de-fence resorted to fire only then when the Versailles troops had already commenced their wholesale murdering of prisoners.

The heroism of children, women and men as they fought to de-fend their "Communal luxury" would live on in the memory of the socialist movement and workers. Fighting and dying became a sign of revolutionary honour. Memoirs often recall scenes like this one from Lissagaray about the barricade of the Faubourg du Temple:

[T]he most indefatigable gunner was a child. The barricade taken, all its defenders were shot, and the child's turn also came. He asked for three minutes' respite; "so that he could take his mother, who lived opposite, his silver watch *in order that she might at least not lose everything*". The officer, invol-untarily moved, let him go. Not thinking to see him again; but three minutes after the child cried, "Here I am!" jumped onto the pavement, and nimbly leant against the wall near the corpses of his comrades.

Lissagaray concluded, "Paris will never die as long as she brings forth such people". And Victor Hugo, who did not originally support the Commune, but responded in solidarity in the face of the massacre, wrote a poem about this incident. He ends with the wishful thought that the officer pardoned the child.

Gustave Courbet recalled:

> The drunkenness of carnage and destruction had taken over this people ordinarily so mild, but so fearsome when pushed to the brink... We will die if we must, shouted men, women and children, but we will not be sent to Cayenne.[4]

Louise Michel became famous for her confrontational stance at her trial:

> Since it seems that every heart which beats for liberty has only right to a little lead, I too demand my part. If you let me live, I shall not cease to cry vengeance... If you are not cowards, kill me.

Out of fear that she would become a martyr around which workers could mobilize, she was condemned to transportation to New Caledonia, where she met Nathalie Lemel. During the defence of Paris, Lemel had taken command of a contingent of the *Union des Femmes*. They marched, red flag in the lead, from a meeting in the *mairie* [town hall] of the fourth arrondissement to defend Les Batignolles. There, the 120 women held back government troops for several hours. Those who were taken were shot on the spot, one of whom was the dressmaker Blanche Lefebvre, an organizer of the *Union des Femmes* and another member of Marx's circle. Some held a barricade on Place Pigalle for a further three hours, but all were killed on what Lissagaray called "this legendary barricade". Lemel cared for the wounded for hours. Her comrade Elisabeth Dmitrieff was at Montmartre with Louise Michel and Léo Frankel in the last hours.

The mass of the poor had few options but to die bravely, which they did with pride. The more educated, if fortunate, found their way into exile. Frankel was smuggled out by a coach driver and escaped to Germany with Dmitrieff. They could be disguised as a Prussian couple because they spoke German fluently. Dmitrieff would return to Russia, only to go into exile in Siberia with a revolutionary with whom she had a genuine marriage. Because of her isolation, she never heard of the amnesty and so lived out the rest of her life in the tundra where so many revolutionaries perished. Michel kept her word and eventually returned to France under the amnesty, was arrested on a demonstration of unemployed workers in 1883 and sentenced to six years of solitary confinement, arrested again in 1890. She returned to France from England, to where she had escaped, and died of pneumonia in January 1905.

A doctor commented on the bravery of the Communards:

> I cannot desire the triumph of your cause; but I have never seen wounded men preserve more calm and sang-froid during operations. I attribute this courage to the energy of their convictions.

And this is how the Commune's supporters interpreted the courageous resistance. It inspired generations, illustrating why the sentiment "it is better to die fighting than to live on your knees" is the most principled response to ruling-class barbarism. If they had meekly surrendered in the name of avoiding violence, there is no ev-

AN ODE TO EMANCIPATION

idence that lives would have been saved, and the revolution would surely not have inspired generations of working-class and socialist activists.

Political assessments

"We'll change henceforth the old conditions" runs a line of Pottier's *Internationale*. But how is it to be done? Which politics and theory related best to the needs of the Commune? When remembering workers' struggles, assessing the political ideas tested in battle is an important part of honouring their memory. If the suffering of the masses in defeat is to be worth the blood spilled, it is the responsibility of those inspired by them to try to learn the lessons, lest their sacrifices be endlessly repeated. In the last article Rosa Luxemburg wrote before being murdered in January 1919, she made reference to the Paris Commune as a metaphor for the fate of the revolution unravelling around her. But, from the perspective of the historic mission of the working class, such defeats served a purpose:

> Where would we be today *without* those "defeats", from which we draw historical experience, understanding, power and idealism?... [W]e stand on the foundation of those very defeats; and we cannot do without *any* of them, because each one contributes to our strength and understanding.

Again and again, in the intervening 150 years, workers have shown that if only they can take control, they would build a humane society, a socialist world. In every struggle we can celebrate the signs of this, and that inspiration unites those of many different politics on the left. Just think. One hundred and fifty years ago, when the fight for women's rights was in its infancy, the more radical clubs in Paris demanded and got support for the right to abortion.

However, the question which has eluded workers so far is how to win control and hold it, how to defeat the powerful forces of capitalism arrayed against them. Proudhonists, Jacobins and Blanquists were the most influential political groups in the Commune Committee. Marx's International had thousands of members, but was far from cohered around his theory and politics. None of these groups could offer the lead required.

The National Guard had elected a Central Committee only a couple of weeks before the uprising. Though inexperienced, they gathered to consider what to do in light of the spontaneous insurrection. By the end of the day the Hôtel de Ville was occupied as the headquarters of the insurgents. But they lacked the confidence to assert their authority and organize the necessary defence and reorganization of the city. In their political confusion, they turned for leadership to the only constitutional body left in Paris, the mayors, who were appointed by the hated central government! The Central Committee of the National Guard insisted that only a newly elected body could take on all the urgent tasks the city confronted. It was eight days before negotiations with the mayors enabled the election of an authoritative body, in which valuable time was lost to the advantage of the Versailles soldiers threatening Paris. Élie Reclus asked on voting day: "What does legality mean at a time of revolution?

Virtually every historian who has written about it comments on the shambolic nature of the National Guard, which ensured that the Versailles government's victory was easier than it should have been. Similarly, most make a point of discussing the Commune's flat-footed response to the mass uprising. Few, however, draw any political conclusions or seriously explain what went wrong. Edwards sums up the reasons for the disaster: the main concern of the majority of the Committee "was to 'legalize' its situation by divesting it-self of the power that had so unexpectedly fallen into its hands". The Blanquists urged a march on Versailles, "a plan which might well have succeeded" following the fraternization between the army and the Guardsmen. Gluckstein argues that Thiers and Co. would never be weaker than in those first hours and days after 18 March 1871. Military discipline had evaporated, and the French army was yet to be buoyed up by prisoners of war released by Bismarck. Supporting this view is the fact that Thiers rejected a request for troops to set up an anti-Commune outfit inside Paris: "Neither 5,000, nor 500, nor five; I need the few troops still available – and in whom I don't yet have full confidence – to defend the government". A Commune supporter reported that in Versailles the regular troops were not even trusted to patrol the streets.

Auguste Blanqui shared with Marx the expectation that the war would create a situation ripe for revolution. But unlike Marx he did not see the working class as the agent to *make* that revolution, only as supporters for a coup. As a result, his supporters had not built roots in working-class organizations or communities, and he languished in jail throughout the revolution due to his involvement in an attempted insurrection just months before. "Blanqui's own account of the debacle [of August 1870] is painfully honest", Gluckstein explains. Blanqui wrote of the response of the workers of Belleville to these gun-toting strangers calling for them to rise up: "[t]he population appeared dumbstruck...held back by fear". And he concluded "We can do nothing without the people!" In spite of their history of organising conspiratorial coups by tiny numbers, the Blanquists participated with great enthusiasm in the mass uprising and the institutions it threw up. Their strength was their prepared-ness to organize and respond with the necessary violence to defeat the murderous forces arrayed against the Commune. However, lacking their most authoritative leader, the Blanquists were defeated in the debate about marching on Versailles, and a critical moment was missed.

Despite their hostility to organization, the Proudhonists took many of the leading positions in the Commune Committee. Their tradition had long cultivated a hostility to political organization of all kinds, which manifested in a reluctance to give elected bodies of the Commune real authority. This then undermined the confidence of those bodies to act decisively, providing Versailles time to get on the offensive. The Proudhonists' respect for private property was also responsible for the decision to leave the enormous wealth of the bourgeoisie safe in the National Bank, and informed a general reticence to take decisive measures in the field of economic and military policy.

Proudhonism today is dead as a political current; however, Proudhon's disciple, Bakunin, still influences some activists. In a typical formulation, Bakunin wrote in his critique of the Commune: "the cause of [humanity's] troubles does not lie in any particular form of government but in the fundamental principles and the very existence of government, whatever form it takes". But this radical-sounding generality obscures the fact that the Commune's troubles came not from an abstract category, but from the very real power of Thiers' counter-revolutionary army. Only an equally organized power based on working-class democracy could have defended the Commune from the massacre that was to come. Bakunin's abstract slogans – which live on in anarchist milieus today – provide absolutely no guide for what to do in the face of the threat posed by the brutal machine that is the bourgeois state. Workers could not – and still cannot – ignore politics and organization.

But it wasn't just the question of defence. The demand of the bakers to end night work raised a lot of debate because Commune

Committee members, influenced by such ideas as Bakunin articulates, refused to issue a decree to abolish night work, even though they supported it. Bakers had been campaigning for two years, hampered by the tiny size of the bakeries which mitigated against effective organization. The Committee's response was ludicrous. They opposed any state action on principle, and argued that the workers should "themselves safeguard their interests in relation to the owners". Benoît Malon represented the views of the bakers, 3,000 of whom marched to the Hôtel de Ville demanding a decree: "until now the state has intervened *against* the interests of workers. It is at least fair that today the state intervene for the workers".

Abstract shibboleths against all organization are no guide to how the left should have related to the radical organizations such as the *Union des Femmes*, the Artists' Federation, and the clubs. If you took these principles seriously you would boycott them, a completely sectarian and destructive attitude which would make you irrelevant, unable to contribute to developing people's consciousness and winning arguments for strategies to win.

It was Marx and Engels who best generalized the lessons of the Commune. Marx had been committed to a view of working-class self-emancipation well before the Commune showed a glimpse of how it could be done. He had witnessed the radical workers' societies and, critically, the Silesian weavers' revolt of 1844, and had subsequently never doubted the creativity and organizational genius of the organized proletariat. His *Theses on Feuerbach* answered the question of how workers could be "educated" for a new society: they educate themselves through their own conscious activity. Marx and Engels developed this idea further in their *German Ideology*, where they argued that to build a socialist society, "the alteration of men on a mass scale is necessary, an alteration which can only take place in a practical movement, a revolution".

Now the Parisian masses had revealed the answer to the question of what to do about the repressive state. Marx had been grappling with this since he concluded in *The Eighteenth Brumaire of Louis Bonaparte* that the problem had been until then that "[a]ll revolutions perfected this machine instead of breaking it" But what could take its place? Two days after *la semaine sanglante,* Marx gave his address to the International, emphasising the achievements of the Commune and its importance to the future of the workers' movement. He had warned against such an uprising in the weeks previous, fearing it was premature, yet did not hesitate to leap to its defence. As with so much of his political work, his writings on the Commune emphasize its fundamental aspects.

Unlike the bourgeois revolutions which primarily benefited a minority of capitalist exploiters, the potential of a workers' revolution to liberate the whole of humanity was now shown in practice. He explains how the democratic structures, with the army and police disbanded and the population armed, were the foundation on which workers can be emancipated from the exploitation of their labour. In this way, the practice of the workers of Paris actually broke new ground; their heroism created the conditions for Marx and Engels to clarify and concretize their previous ideas regarding the self-emancipation of the working class. Overall, Marx's writings on the Commune stand in sharp contrast to the abstract shibboleths in Bakunin's work.

But it would be Lenin who brought all these elements together, transcending what is usually assumed to be a contradiction between spontaneous revolts and organization.[5] The counterposition between spontaneity and organization abounds in Bakunin's critique, and is taken for granted by many activists today. The issue is particularly fraught when women are involved. Women's activities in rebellions like this are often portrayed as elemental, unplanned and not very political. This emphasis on spontaneity is often sexist and downplays the role of leadership, foresight and planning by the women themselves. The Commune perfectly illustrates Lenin's arguments. To begin with, there can be no revolution without spontaneity. The radicalization sufficient to generate the Paris Commune did not develop incrementally, it exploded and shocked the world. It's true that the uprising that seized the cannon in Montmartre emerged in a context of rising discontent and bitterness, but the rebellion in turn radicalized and transformed the situation decisively.

The Commune shows how there is not some barrier between a revolutionary upsurge itself and the activities and politics that exist beforehand. For instance Eugène Varlin and Nathalie Lemel were involved in workers' campaigns for women's rights and equal pay in the 1860s. In the growing number of strikes before 1871, some workers had learnt from their experiences. A strike by 5,000 bronze workers in 1867 won with support from the International, which organized funds from workers in other countries. The lesson of international solidarity was not forgotten. And other workers – significantly in textiles from where women participated in Dmitrieff's *Union des Femmes* – began to see the value of organization and strikes in a number of cities. In a strike by miners in the Loire region workers' wives had fought bravely against the gendarmes during a strike at Le Creusot in 1870.

Ideas promoted by the Proudhonists, who argued that "women should stay indoors and avoid the physical and moral dangers of workshops", were now rejected by working-class men. They declared that women should exercise their independence and "will march alongside us in the exercise of democratic and social cooperation". Those ideas could most effectively be kept alive and popularised if taken up by organizations, rather than being left to the whimsy of individual happenstance.

Lenin's most significant theoretical breakthrough was to see that the task for revolutionaries is to prepare for the spontaneous outbursts before they happen. This preparation is not a purely intellectual exercise, but entails participating in every struggle, raising ideas which challenge participants to reject the ideas of capitalism. Not all workers will develop class consciousness at the same time; consciousness will always be uneven, as it was in the Commune.

This means revolutionaries need to build a party which organizes the most class-conscious and militant workers, the "vanguard" as Lenin called them. Such a revolutionary party needs to raise the level of class consciousness generally, by which Lenin meant the degree to which workers understand the role of their own class, and that of all other social layers, and how much they understand their class power. They need to understand that their class can and must lead other classes in a revolution if capitalism is to be overthrown. The party needs a history of participating in and leading struggles so they gain a wide understanding of the momentum of struggle, how to judge different strategies and the arguments of different political organizations. Only this offers the best chance that the arguments of those who always support compromise and moderation will be defeated.

The vanguard must have burned into their consciousness that if our side seriously challenges the ruling class and their state, there is no limit to their "undisguised savagery and lawless revenge", in Marx's words. Revolutions have time and again crashed against the seemingly timeless existence of the state, and the mistake of seeking to remain within the "rule of law".

Lenin's solution was to organize the vanguard to be prepared to repeat the first acts of the Commune: to disband the police and army, and to arm the working class and poor. It must not shrink from responding to ruling-class violence in order to defend the revolution.

The Commune's legacy

In the Paris Commune, the ruling class saw the shape of a new society. They understood that such a world of equality and justice could only be built on the ruins of capitalism. So they sought to systematically obliterate its memory.

In the Louvre today, images of the royal family overthrown in the Great Revolution are sympathetically portrayed. But a small collection from the Commune is hidden away in the basement. A collection of artefacts, documents and the like is included in the museum dedicated to the art of Paul Éluard in Saint-Denis. Ironically it is housed in an old Carmelite convent. It was originally set up by the Communist council of Saint-Denis.

In the 1870s the bourgeoisie set out to refashion Paris with monuments to the Republic. The last quarter of the nineteenth century has been referred to as "a golden age of monument building" as part of the effort at "self-definition" following the trauma of 1870-71. Restoring the Vendôme column was, of course, a huge priority. Sometimes the purpose of new monuments or buildings was made explicit. The church of Sacré-Coeur was built on Montmartre. When laying the foundation stone, architect Charles Rohault de Fleury declared that Sacré-Coeur reclaimed for the nation "the place chosen by Satan and where was accomplished the first act of that horrible Saturnalia".

It is easy to see the negation of the Commune in the grotesque splendour of the Sacré-Coeur. But a lot of the reconstruction was not so explicit. Much of the art which was promoted and the spaces reorganized were merely presented as celebrations of the Republic. But try as they may, the memory often reverberated in what was not said or built. One space allowed to socialists was the *Mur des Fédérés* (Wall of the Federals), located in the *Père Lachaise* cemetery where the blood of unknown numbers was spilled in the last days of the Commune. Presumably authorities thought this the most fitting memorial: calculated to sear our souls and to signal that attempts at anti-capitalist rebellions will always be drowned in unimaginable savagery. But they were mistaken. Visitors leave a constant sea of red roses, and leave with a renewed hatred of the bourgeoisie and a desire to fight for the promise of the Commune. In 1907, the Parisian municipal council planned to install Paul Vautier-Moreau's *Monument to the Victims of Revolutions*, sculpted from the stones of the barricades, on which was engraved Victor Hugo's clarion call to end the "vengeance". There was such an outcry from supporters of the Commune, who preferred to keep that space simply for the Communards, that it had to be placed outside the wall of the cemetery.

William Morris paid homage to the destruction of the Vendôme column in his novel *News from Nowhere*, published in 1890. The apricot orchard which replaces Trafalgar Square, dominated by the statue of Admiral Nelson is, as Ross says, a "symbolic revisioning [of] both the Place Vendôme and Trafalgar Square...their aesthetic of nationalistic and timeless monumentality become supra-national space".

In spite of the efforts of the descendants of the butchers who saturated Paris in blood, the memory of this first workers' revolution cannot be completely suppressed. So a social history of Paris, published in English in 2010, revisits some of the accounts by its participants and supporters. Eric Hazan, the author, reminds us how modern day charlatans, rather than obscure the history completely, cynically attempt to co-opt the inspiration of the Commune for their own opportunistic reasons. A plaque in Paris has inscribed on it: "The last barricade of the Commune resisted in the Rue de la Fontaine-au-Roi. A hundred and twenty years later, the Socialist party and its first secretary Pierre Mauroy render homage to the people of Paris who sought to change their lives, and to the 30,000 dead of the Time of the Cherries". Hazan, who documents the truth of those days, reminds us: "This trumpery makes short work of history, for Louis Blanc, the Mauroy of his day, maintained that 'this insurrection is completely to be condemned, and must be condemned by any true republican'." *Le Temps des Cerises* to which the inscription refers is a song written in 1866. It became popular during the Commune, with verses added as it was sung on the barricades and in the clubs. The title is a metaphor for the hope for a new life after a revolution, making the hypocritical inscription by the reformist party even more galling.

For decades workers remembered the Communards' courageous defiance. On May Day 1901, thousands of mourners joined the funeral procession for Paule Mincke through the streets of Paris. They chanted "Vive la Commune!" and "Vive l'Internationale!" as more than 600 police, 500 soldiers and 100 cavalry guarded the streets against any possibility of a repeat of 1871. More than 100,000 attended Louise Michel's funeral in Paris in 1905.

Socialists and anarchists celebrated the Commune every March. The ghastly images of tortured women beamed around the world by the bourgeois press could not undercut the sense of pride and solidarity that their courage inspired. In the New South Wales outback mining city of Broken Hill, for at least a decade into the twentieth century, the Socialist Sunday School organized the annual anniversary commemoration of the Commune.

In another piece I concluded that "[it] certainly was not portrayed as a celebration of male achievements, as is often claimed by feminist historians: 'What greater and grander sublimity can be depicted than that of men and women who are prepared to sacrifice their lives for even a dream?'" An article in the socialist paper in the town "emphasized female bravery", telling the story of when soldiers tried to force Communards to kneel before their guns: "one woman with a child in her arms refused to do so, shouting to her companions: 'Show these wretches that you know how to die upright'." An historian of the annual events which continued for decades writes:

> They drew on the Commune as an example of international cooperation, drawing on their shared class identity. The Commune was rewritten annually, creating a palimpsest. Speakers drew on the Commune as a symbol of working-class government, or of revolution, a symbol of warning and hope, of past, present and future, something to learn from, and revere.

In spite of so many efforts to obscure its history, the Commune is still invoked as a reference point for the idea of revolution, or challenges to authority to this very day. A post by *Buzzfeed*, "Stormings of History Ranked from Best to Worst", appeared in response to the invasion of the Capitol by far-right Trump supporters. The Commune is their second-best example, second only to the October Revolution. Even the prestigious *Lancet,* on the 150th anniversary pays homage to the Commune with an article about Mary Putnam Jacobi. The conclusion is a tribute to the power of the Commune to inspire hope for a better world: "The origins of her philosophy, a philosophy that provides the seed for an American renaissance today, lay in the blood spilt on the streets of Paris 150 years ago".

Conclusion

We began with the image of the "sphinx" conjured by Marx to convey how the Commune terrified the bourgeoisie and their hangers-on. We leave it as the world descends into ever more horrifying chaos which creates catastrophes one after the other. The World Bank warns governments around the globe to avoid making premature cuts to measures taken to prevent the economy from completely collapsing. This advice is not driven by humanitarian concern for those who would suffer from the cuts, but by fear of revolt. The sphinx haunts them still.

The Paris Commune reminds *us* of what Walter Benjamin said, that the fine and spiritual aspects of life we hunger for can only be won by the struggle for the rough, material things which make them possible. And that "they are present as confidence, as courage, as humour, as cunning, as steadfastness in this struggle". That is why the Paris Commune still commands our attention, and is worthy of serious study. And why it still has the power to inspire our confidence in the working class to create a "Communal luxury" for humanity to this day.

Notes

1. The International included this grouping, but also Proud-honists, who dominated the French section, Blanquists and others.
2. Many revolutionary women escaped the stifling pressure from their families by entering a "white marriage" in which the man expected no sexual relationship.
3. Quoted in Gluckstein 2006, p49. Lissagaray uses *oriflamme* for scarlet banner which, in its literary meaning, denotes a principle or ideal that serves as a rallying point in a struggle.
4. The notorious penal colony in French Guiana.
5. For my assessment of Lenin, see Bloodworth 2013.

9

An ode to emancipation which crosses time

INTERVIEW WITH OLIVIER BESANCENOT

Olivier Besancenot and Michael Löwy published *Marx a Paris, 1871: le chair bleu de Jenny* (Paris: Le Temps des Cerises, 2021). The English version, *Marx in Paris 1871,* is scheduled for publication by Haymarket in March 2022. Julien Salingue for *l'Anticapitaliste* talked to Olivier Besancenot about the book.

For this book, you have chosen a rather original format, since it is a political fiction, recounting a visit by Marx to Paris during the Commune. Why did you make this choice?

It followed a discussion with Michael, and I think it was Michael who came up with the idea first, with the goal of doing something a little out of step with what has already been done and which will be repeated on the occasion of the 150th anniversary of the Commune. Basically, it was a question of finding something striking, original, to illustrate Marx's thinking on the Paris Commune.

We therefore imagined this clandestine, improbable journey of Marx, led by his daughter Jenny, within the Commune itself, with meetings with some of its leading figures, in order to bring out Marx's political thinking on the Commune. It is actually remarkable to see how his ideas emerged in the heat of the action. A pertinent immediate analysis (the Call to the International), but also a political, strategic, global questioning. This is one of Marx's great strengths: to be able to understand that from the unfolding of events themselves can be born a process of emancipation that has not necessarily been imagined on paper, in think tanks, or even in the offices of the International. Marx's writings on this famous force of emancipation that was finally found when he speaks of the Commune, were extremely advanced in relation to a whole range of sectors of the workers' movement, the revolutionary movement, with intonations that are even sometimes more libertarian than those of some libertarians. A reflection on emancipation, on confrontation with the state apparatus, on the need to build forms of political, democratic sovereignty...

Exactly. To put it in a very synthetic way: what did the Commune change for Marx?

I would say that it was the idea that it is not enough for the state apparatus to change hands, from a social class point of view, in order to change the nature of the state. It is an oppressive system, a boa constrictor, to use Marx's phrase, which stifles civil society and democracy. And that therefore it must be extinguished, that we should go towards the extinction of the state, and that one of the possible avenues for this extinction was shown by the policies of the Commune in action: revocability of elected officials, a cap on the remuneration of elected officials and magistrates, etc. All these concrete policies that call into question the heart of the bureaucracy that is the state apparatus. And with the Commune there was a beginning of extinction, which could not really be fully illustrated because of the duration of the Commune [72 days], but was a glimpse of the future all the same. Marx immediately understood that and immediately analysed it. And this would have an impact on Marx's thinking, on the debates and the culture of the workers' movement in general.

Marx followed all the debates, what was happening in the world, the social and political situations, and while he had not imagined that the insurrection would come from Paris, he delved into the analysis of the Commune, immediately, although he had been a little caught off guard and was at the time immersed in reflection on the analysis of the capitalist system and its crises. And his strength was to produce analyses as events unfolded, to grasp their scope.

To bring all this to life, you imagine encounters between Marx and certain personalities of the Commune, in Paris, during the insurrection. Looking at them we notice a significant presence of women: Louise Michel, Elisabeth Dmitrieff, Nathalie Lemel, but also of course Jenny Marx who accompanies her father. Is it from a desire on your part to highlight in particular the role of women in the Paris uprising?

It was not necessarily theorized and constructed, but we realized, as we looked at real figures, that women played a central role in the social and political history of the Commune. This was the case from the start of the uprising, with the protection of the guns against their potential takeover by the Versaillais in the streets of Montmartre, at the call of the vigilance committee of the citizens of Montmartre, around Louise Michel in particular. But it was also the role and the place taken by women, against the zeitgeist of the time, because machismo was present, even within the International and in the various revolutionary clubs.

A revolutionary event like the Commune – but this applies to all revolutionary events – is the outpouring of phenomena that have been simmering in society for months and months, or even longer. This was the case in Paris, with in particular a multitude of revolutionary clubs in which women became more and more involved. We can also think of the siege of Paris by the Prussians, during which Nathalie Lemel was, with the cooperative "La Ménagère" and the restaurant "La Marmite" at the centre of popular solidarity and mutual aid, coming to the aid of almost 10,000 Parisians who were dying of hunger.

So the Women's Union, which was formed in the eye of the storm of the Commune, was the product of all this previous work, and when Élisabeth Dmitrieff (representative of the International) arrived and participated in the founding of the Women's Union, much of the activity was already underway, entrenched.

It is true that when we think of "the women of the Commune", it is the figure of Louise Michel who comes most often to mind, sometimes, often even, "forgetting" Elisabeth Dmitrieff. This is not the case in your book, where she occupies an important place, commensurate with her role during the Commune.

It is true that she is less well known than Louise Michel, and that she remains a name that evokes something, but we do not really know what. However, her name, beyond the feminist struggle, the struggle for women's rights in the heart of the Commune, with the Women's Union, is also associated with self-management. Elisabeth Dmitrieff and her actions represent one of the first examples of self-management on this scale.

Dmitrieff influenced the Commune as much as she was the product of it. She was a young Russian immigrant who became completely caught up in the story of Chernychevsky's novel *What is to be done?*. A novel whose heroine emancipates herself from her own milieu – made up of arranged marriages – and draws inspiration from the traditional forms of pooling of goods and production that existed in some localities of the Russian peasantry, known as *obchchina*, and transposes it to workers' cooperatives. Reading this novel inflamed Elisabeth Dmitrieff, she emancipated herself from her milieu, politicized herself, especially alongside political refugees in Switzerland where she met Marxists, then went to London and met Marx, discussed with him... Kristin Ross talks about all this in *Communal Luxury: The Political Imaginary of the Paris Commune*. And when she arrived Marx appreciated her and took her into consideration, to the point of sending her as his emissary to Paris during the Commune, so that she could be his eyes and ears.

After a few days she found herself at the head of the Women's Union, alongside Nathalie Lemel and others, and her first project, which she discussed with Leo Frankel, was to form self-managed workers' cooperatives, where the workers would pay themselves, to make for example fabrics for sandbags for the ramparts or uniforms for the National Guard. So Dmitrieff also represented an experience that was unfortunately also aborted because of the short duration of the Commune.

How did you choose the different characters Marx encounters in your book? Did you try to fix criteria to give an "overview" or did these characters impose themselves?

We didn't make a cast list, we did it instinctively, I think. As we do each time we write together, Michael and I shared out the chapters, and then the names imposed themselves, added together… The question we asked ourselves, because it is the limit of the genre, was the risk of redoing a history of the Commune a little too much "from above", with names that we already knew. But what guided us were Marx's writings on the Commune, so we were obliged to follow the thread of the political relations that Marx had, often remotely, at the time, and thus to have him discuss with these personalities.

So to sum up, a book on the Commune, on Marx's thought, but also a book that is meant to say things about current events?

The Commune is an ode to emancipation which speaks through time, and a good reminder when we face all the wrongs of bureaucracy.

It is also a way of resourcing ourselves in internationalism. Because yes, the Commune was born from a popular uprising against the siege, the advance of Bismarck's troops, and the will to win the war. But among the great figures of the Commune, as well as among the anonymous Communards, there were thousands and thousands of exiles, often political, but also economic : Prussian, Italian, Polish, Russian… The Commune was an internationalist act.

And it is also a way of remembering that our political history did not begin with the Russian Revolution of 1917. It has previous roots, and all the debates that irrigated the international workers' movement following the crushing of the Commune, emphasizing in particular what the Communards had failed to do – seizing the Bank of France, marching on Versailles, etc. – make it possible to understand what the political obsessions of the Bolsheviks were. We understand better the famous dance in the snow of Lenin on the day when the Russian revolution had "held" for a day longer than the Commune.

Across time, the Commune is not only its failures, but a source of living inspiration, the first experience of popular emancipation and power, of the power of the exploited and oppressed, with all its limitations, but which speaks to us across the decades. And we realize that, 150 years later, it is an unresolved matter with the powers that be: the Commune still does not have a good press in the thinking of the ruling class, and we see to what point the attitudes that produced Versailles have not disappeared.

10

The Paris Commune of 1871, banks and debt

ERIC TOUSSAINT

On the occasion of the 150th anniversary of the extraordinary experience of the Paris Commune, it is fundamental to draw a number of lessons from it. The measures a government takes regarding its Central Bank, the debts of working class people, public debt and private banks are decisive. If a popular government does not implement radical financial measures, it will be responsible for ending in failure, with possibly tragic consequences for the population. The Commune, an extraordinary and dramatic experiment, exemplifies this, and must thus be analysed from this point of view.

The role of debt in the emergence of the Paris Commune

It was the desire of the reactionary government to pay off its debt to Prussia and continue to repay existing public debts that precipitated the Commune experiment. Let us recall that it was Louis Bonaparte (Napoleon III) who declared war on Prussia in July 1870 and that that military venture soon ended in a total fiasco. The Prussian Army beat the French Army in early September 1870, and imprisoned Napoleon III in Sedan, triggering the fall of the Second Empire followed by the proclamation of the Republic. The payment of 5 billion francs was the condition laid down by Bismarck for signing the peace treaty and withdrawing the forces of occupation.

In a document adopted in solidarity with the Commune on 30 May 1871 by the leadership of the International Workingmen's Association also known as the First International), Karl Marx emphasizes the enormous burden of public debt that had benefited the French bourgeoisie and weighed heavily on Thiers' "republican" government that had replaced Napoleon III's: "The Second Empire had more than doubled the national debt, and plunged all the large towns into heavy municipal debts.

The war had fearfully swelled the liabilities, and mercilessly ravaged the resources of the nation. To that, Marx adds the expenses incurred by the maintenance of half a million Prussian soldiers on French soil, the 5 billion francs of compensation demanded by Bismarck and 5 per cent interest to be added to that amount in case of delayed payment.

Who was to repay the debt?

Then Marx asks, "Who was to pay this bill?" He replies that from the point of view of the bourgeoisie and Thiers himself, it could only be done by brutally crushing the people, "that the appropriators of wealth could hope to shift onto the shoulders of its producers the cost of a war which they, the appropriators, had themselves originated." According to Marx, Thiers' government was convinced that the only way to make the people of France agree to being bled dry to repay the public debt would be to start a civil war, overcome their resistance and force them to foot the bill. Bismarck shared this opinion and was convinced that to bring France to heel and get them to agree to fulfil the conditions laid down by victorious Prussia, the people needed to be crushed, starting with those of Paris. However he did not wish to use the exhausted Prussian Army to do this. He wanted Thiers to do the dirty work. Thiers had tried and failed to persuade Bismarck to send his troops into Paris. In order to carry on repaying the national debt which profited the bourgeoisie and to start repaying the war debt, Thiers proceeded to borrow 2 billion francs in the weeks running up to the Commune.[1]

To put down the people of Paris who were armed, Thiers mounted a military operation on 18 March 1871 to steal 400 of their cannons and machine guns. It was the failure of this attempt that led to popular mobilization and ended up with Thiers' government fleeing and setting up in Versailles. Those in charge of the Communards made the mistake of not pursuing Thiers and his government. They should have fetched him from Versailles, detained him and thus prevented the government from regrouping their troops and sending them out later against the people of Paris and the other cities which took part in the uprising.

From Versailles, in the following days and weeks, Thiers organized the crushing of the Communes as soon as they emerged in different parts of France (Marseille, Lyon, Narbonne, Saint-Etienne, Toulouse, Le Creusot, Limoges...).While he used the part of the Army he had at his disposal to put down the Communes in the South of France, Thiers pretended to negotiate with the Paris Commune to gain time and create the conditions for a final offensive against it.

This led to a delegation from Thiers' government being sent to Frankfurt at the beginning of May 1871 to ask Bismarck for help in crushing the Paris Commune. Bismarck replied that they should first pay the instalments due on the debt and that to help them create the right conditions for victory, he would allow Thiers to use the part of the French Army that the Prussians were holding prisoner to attack Paris. Bismarck also agreed to send part of the Prussian troops as back-up though they were not to enter Paris. Finally, after long negotiations, Bismarck agreed to wait until the Paris Commune had been dealt with before receiving the first payment. This was the plan concocted between the French government and the Prussian leader that finally overcame the Paris Commune.

The remainder of this article concentrates on the Commune's policy regarding rent and the debts of the working classes on the one hand, and the Bank of France on the other.

The Commune's positive measures dealing with rent and other debts

On 29 March 1871, the Commune decided to suspend payment of rent, including rent owed since October 1870. Another measure taken on the same day in favour of the people was to ban pawn-brokers from selling pawned items.[2] Pawn-shops (known as *Monts-de-Piété*) were private bodies that made their profit from secure loans using personal property as collateral.[3] Should a person who had deposited an item in exchange for a loan not repay their debt, the pawn-broker was entitled to sell the pawned object. There were over a million objects accumulated in the pawn-shops.

After a particularly harsh winter, poor households had pawned eighty thousand blankets in order to borrow money to buy food. 73% of pawned items belonged to working people. Of one and a half million loans in a year, two thirds, that is one million, were loans of just 3 to 10 francs.

At the end of April 1871, after long debates between moderates and radicals, the Commune decided that people who had acquired a secured loan of less than 20 francs could recover their goods free of charge. The most radical elected representatives, like Jean-Baptiste Clément, author of famous songs including *Le Temps des Cerises* and *La Semaine Sanglante*, considered that the Commune should have done more, more quickly, in dealing with pawn-shops and other aspects of the living conditions of the working classes.[4]

Among those advocating a very moderate approach regarding working-class and middle-class debt (which affected a huge number of small shop-keepers and artisans) was Charles Beslay, the oldest member of the 1871 Commune, a disciple and close friend of Proudhon. Beslay systematically stood up in defence of Finance and creditors. He will be mentioned further on in the section devoted to the Commune's policy regarding the Bank of France.

However, mention should be made of the Commune's decisions on 25 April to requisition empty housing for the victims of bombing by the troops of Versailles, then on 28 April to forbid employers from levying fines and making deductions from wages.[5]

The Paris Commune made a fatal error in not taking control of the Bank of France

The headquarters of the Bank of France, its principal reserves and its governing body were situated in Paris Commune territory. The leadership of the Paris Commune made the grave error of not taking it over, which would have been absolutely justified.

In his *Histoire de la Commune de 1871* published in 1876, Prosper-Olivier Lissagaray, a militant intellectual who participated in the Communards' street fighting, criticized the Commune's leaders who were "mesmerized in front of the haute bourgeoisie's cash-box ie the Bank of France when they had it in their hands".

The Commune's only demand from the Bank of France was to receive the financial advances they needed to maintain a balanced budget while still paying wages to the National Guardsmen. Paris's National Guard was a citizens' militia in charge of law and order and of military defence. It consisted of 300,000 armed personnel for Paris's population of two million.

Thiers' reactionary government, in collusion with the Prussian occupier, received 20 times more cash than the Commune.

The Bank of France barely loosened its purse-strings in response to the financial needs of the Commune whilst it extensively financed those who wanted to crush the people of Paris and put a hasty end to the social revolution. During the two months of the Commune experiment, Thiers' reactionary government, in collusion with the Prussian occupier, received 20 times more cash than the Commune.[6]

Karl Marx thought that the Commune had been wrong not to get hold of the Bank of France: "The appropriation of the Bank of France alone would have been enough to dissolve all the pretensions of the Versailles people into terror." He wrote that had the Bank been requisitioned, "[W]ith a small amount of sound common sense, however, they could have reached a compromise with Versailles useful to the whole mass of the people - the only thing that could be achieved at that time."

In Lissagaray's words, "the Commune could not see the real hostages it could have taken: the Bank of France, the Real Estate Register (Enregistrement et les Domaines), the State bank handling official deposits or CDC (Caisse des dépôts et consignations), etc."

In 1891, Frederick Engels similarly wrote:

> The most difficult thing to understand is, indeed, the sacred respect with which the Commune reverently stopped before the portals of the Bank of France. This was also a portentous political error. The Bank in the hands of the Commune – that was worth more than ten thousand hostages. It would have meant the pressure of the entire French bourgeoisie on the Versailles government in the interests of peace with the Commune.

The leaders of the Paris Commune essentially enabled the Bank of France to finance their own enemies – that is, the conservative government of Thiers at Versailles and its army, which would crush their movement. As we shall see, the Bank of France also financed the Prussian army of occupation that was at the gates of Paris.

Sequence of events concerning the Bank of France and an attempted explanation

In forming an opinion on the attitude of the Commune toward the Bank of France, I have relied mainly on two narratives – the one already cited in this article by Prosper-Olivier Lissagaray, who was a firm partisan of the cause of the Commune, and that of Maxime du Camp, an anti-Communard author whose reactionary writings were to earn him election as a member of the *Académie Française* in 1880. The two authors provide many details on the behaviour of the various protagonists, and despite the fact their points of view are diametrically opposed, their narrative is largely in agreement.

Let's go through the timeline.

On 18 March, Thiers, his government and his administration fled to Versailles. A few days later Gustave Rouland, governor of the Bank of France, joined them in order to be of service, leaving the vice-governor of the bank, Marquis Alexandre De Plœuc, and his administration in Paris. Among Rouland's entourage in Versailles were the regents of the Bank of France, who included Baron Alphonse de Rothschild, owner of the Banque Rothschild, the Bank of France's largest shareholder.

Gustave Rouland tried to convince Thiers to attack the Paris Commune immediately, but Thiers felt it was best to stall for time.

Meanwhile, on 30 March 1871, the Commune had appointed the Proudhonian Charles Beslay as its representative at the Bank of France. Beslay summed up his actions in a letter to the right-wing daily *Le Figaro*, published 13 March 1873: "I went to the Bank with the intention of preserving it from any violence on the part of the radical elements of the Commune, and it is my conviction that I have saved for my country the establishment that was our last financial resource."

Charles Beslay had been elected to the Commune's Council on 26 March 1871 and was its oldest member. He had also been a member of the First International (IWA) since 1866. He had great influence in the Commune. Yet Beslay had a capitalist past: he had founded a factory that employed 200 men and women, which in the mid-19th century was a large company.

Lissagaray, who had lived through the events of the Commune and had studied the minutes of the sessions of the Commune's Council, writes that Beslay, from the start, accepted the position defended by the Marquis de Plœuc, which was that the Commune could not appoint the governor of the Bank of France. It was limited to having a delegate, who was Beslay himself. Lissagaray tells us that "Beslay, deeply moved, hurried off to the Executive Commission, repeated his lesson all the better that he believed it and prided himself on his financial lore. 'The bank,' he said, 'is the fortune of the country: without it, no more industry, no more commerce. If you violate it, all its notes will be so much waste-paper.'" This pessimistic and paralysing conviction was held by a majority within the leadership of the Commune, and its effects were to be tragic.

As Georges Beisson writes: "During its 72 days of existence, the Commune received 16.7 million francs: the 9.4 million that the City of Paris had in its account and 7.3 million that were actually lent by the bank. Meanwhile the Versailles received 315 million francs [...] from the Bank of France," or nearly 20 times as much.

The reactionary Maxime du Camp agrees when he writes that "Whilst the Commune was harassing the Bank of France in Paris for a few thousand-franc notes, the Bank of France was giving millions to the legal government. The troops were arriving, forming units and organizing, and there was no shortage of wages for them." The troops Du Camp is referring to are the ones raised by Thiers, with Bismarck's aid, to destroy the people of Paris. As Du Camp adds, "When Thiers needed money, he informed Rouland, who sent a telegraphic dispatch, and the money arrived."

The Commune had an urgent need of funds to aid the population and to strengthen its defence against imminent attack, but its representatives Beslay and Jourde settled for a pittance. And yet in the vaults of the Bank's head office in Paris there were banknotes, coins, bullion and financial securities worth approximately three billion francs.

Right until the end, the Commune allowed the executives of the Bank of France to have their own, heavily armed militia. The Marquis de Plœuc had several hundred persons under his command who had at their disposal inside the Bank an arsenal made up of hundreds of rifles and ammunition to withstand a siege. Had the Commune actually wished to do so it could have disarmed this militia without firing a shot. But Beslay was totally opposed to the idea.

Maxime du Camp also writes that the Bank's governor, Rouland, had sent the following message to the bank's employees: "Please give precise instructions for banknotes to be made available to the Germans, and also some cash for paying their troops." The Bank of France handed money over to the Prussian occupiers to help them destroy the Commune. Du Camp explains that the Marquis de Plœuc told Jourde, the second delegate of the Commune to the Bank, a boldfaced lie. Du Camp reconstitutes a dialogue between them based on first-hand reports:

> You think us rich,' said M. de Plœuc, 'but we are not; you know very well that when the German troops were marching on Paris, we sent all our holdings away; they have not returned. I am not fooling you; the transfers are easy to track [...] and you will be convinced that the majority of our fortune is in the provinces.' - 'God! Monsieur le Marquis,' Jourde answered, 'I know that very well, but if you advance me the money, the Bank will be protecting itself and helping me to save it, which would be impossible without it.

Within the Commune, supporters of Auguste Blanqui (who was imprisoned by the Thiers government), including Raoul Rigault, were increasingly unhappy with the policy adopted by Beslay, assisted by Jourde and supported by the majority, and on 12 May 1871 they decided to act and attempted to move on the Bank of France with two companies of the National Guard. But Beslay successfully stepped in in extremis to protect the bank and prevent the seizure.

Maxime du Camp concludes: "In this matter old Beslay was really beyond reproach." This abortive attempt by the Blanqui camp had been conceived as a sort of coup and was not part of a coherent vision aimed at enabling the Commune to use the Bank of France to organize its defence and finance a development plan.

Of course the Bank would have had to be taken over "militarily", but it had to be done for a purpose, and the Blanquistes did not know exactly what that purpose was. They did not propose in the Commune's Council (where they held seats) that the Bank of France be taken over and used in the service of a plan for resistance and development. They limited their efforts to attempting to take the Bank by surprise, which did not work since the Blanqui faction did not have arguments for overcoming Beslay's opposition. And so the initiative turned into a fiasco. Note that taking over the Bank of France "militarily" does not mean using artillery, machine guns and rifles. What it does mean is making the decision, at the level of the leadership of the Commune, to take over control of the Bank and remove its governor and vice-governor, bring in a sufficient number of battalions of the National Guard to surround the Bank and demand that its armed occupants lay down their weapons.

The imbalance between the forces and the certainty of the Bank's occupants that they would lose the battle if they resisted would have been enough to ensure their docility. They would have had no hope of reinforcements, at least until the start of the "Bloody Week" on 21 May. The Commune should have taken control of the Bank of France during the first days of its existence.

The Commune had every intention of issuing its own currency, and did have currency issued at the Paris Mint – the Hôtel des Monnaies on the Quai Conti –, but it lacked the gold and silver ingots that were stored at the Bank of France. And there again the Bank's officials were able to count on Beslay's aid in seeing to it that only miniscule quantities of precious metals were released to be struck into coins.

Maxime du Camp explains that the officials of the Bank of France were so afraid that the radical elements of the Commune would win out over Beslay that they moved everything they could into the cellars of the bank in Paris and packed the only stairway leading down there with sand. The operation took place on 20 May and took some 15 hours. Once all the ingots, coinage, notes, securities and ledgers had been moved into two rooms below ground protected by twelve locks, the spiral stairway leading to the rooms was packed with sand and a slab was laid over it. The officials of the Bank of France were so afraid of the Commune that they moved all the currency and securities underground and packed the stairway in sand.

The following day, the Bloody Week began, and ended in the defeat of the people of Paris on 28 May 1871. After the Commune was crushed, Beslay was one of the only Communard leaders (and possibly the only one) who was not executed, sentenced *in absentia*, imprisoned or exiled. The Commune's murderers allowed him to go to Switzerland to settle the inheritance of one of his sisters who had died in August 1870, and on 9 December 1872 charges against him were dismissed by the 17th War Council. Towards the end of his life in Switzerland he also served as executor of Proudhon's will.

The Commune's attitude toward the Bank of France can be explained by the limitations inherent in the strategy of its majority factions – that is, advocates of Proudhon and of Blanqui. Proudhon, who had died in 1865, was not able to take part directly in the decisions, but his supporters were influential. Beslay was far from being the only one. Proudhon, and later his followers, were opposed to having a people's government take control of the Bank of France. Further, they were against expropriating the capitalist banks; their priority was the creation of credit unions. The role they played, via Beslay, was frankly obstructive. The supporters of the intransigent

Auguste Blanqui were also numerous, and had no specific position as to what needed to be done concerning the Bank of France and the role it should have played in a revolutionary government.

Few of the militants were inspired by the ideas of Karl Marx, even if some of them, such as Léo Frankel, did hold responsibilities and were in regular contact with Marx, who was then living in London. Frankel was a member of the *Commission du travail et de l'échange* (Committee for Labour and Exchanges). We might also mention Charles Longuet, who like Frankel was a member of the la *Commission du travail et de l'échange*; Auguste Serraillier, a member of the same Commission; and Elisabeth Dmitrieff, who during the Commune was co-founder of the Women's Union for the Defence of Paris and Aid to the Wounded.

A government of the people must adopt a radical solution regarding the central bank, public debt and private bank

The policy adopted by Beslay is highly relevant today. If a government of the people limits itself to proposing or implementing credit unions (cooperative banks) while maintaining the central bank as it functions today in the State, without socializing the banking sector through expropriation of capitalists, nothing will change at the structural level. If public debt is not radically reduced, the new government will have no real leverage for financing major changes.

Lessons from the Paris Commune

Marx and Engels drew several lessons from the Commune. The need to destroy the capitalist State headed the list. Democratic operation of the government and popular representation with revocability of all delegates was another. A refusal to take a sacrosanct attitude toward finance is a third: a popular government must take control of the central bank and change the nature of property relations in the entire financial sector, which implies expropriating the capitalists. A fourth lesson is closely related to the third: the need to cancel public debt. As a matter of fact, a few years after the Commune, Marx – who participated in writing the programme of the *Parti Ouvrier* (Workers' Party) in France – spoke of the need for "Suppression of the public debt".[7]

The resolute action taken by Soviet Russia and the Cuban revolution regarding the central bank, banks and debt

The Bolsheviks in Russia and the Cuban revolutionaries had learned these lessons and took the necessary measures in 1917–1918, in the case of the decrees adopted by the Soviets, and in 1959–1960 in the case of the Cuban revolution. The government of the Bolsheviks, allied with the Left Socialist-Revolutionaries with the support of the workers', peasants' and soldiers' councils (Soviets) took control of the central bank, issued their own currency, expropriated the bankers, cancelled the peasants' debts and repudiated all debt contracted by the Tsarist regime.[8]

The revolutionary Cubans took control of the central bank, placed Che Guevara at its head, issued their own currency and cancelled public debt. As regards the right to housing, they went much farther than the Commune, and also decreed that tenants should be allowed to continue occupying their living quarters without paying rent.[9] The Bolsheviks also implemented a solution to the problem of housing and related indebtedness.

The lessons of the Paris Commune have been largely forgotten

If a government of the people limits itself to proposing or implementing credit unions (cooperative banks) while maintaining the central bank as it now functions in the contemporary State, without socializing the banking sector through expropriation of capitalists, nothing will change at the structural level. In a broader sense, the lessons of the Paris Commune have been largely forgotten. First, Social Democracy, after its betrayal of internationalism at the start of the First World War, became an instrument of capitalist and imperialist domination; then, dictatorial bureaucratic and Stalinist regimes, with the restoration of capitalism, perpetuated brutal forms of coercion and exploitation.

More recently, progressive regimes in Latin America at the start of the 21st century remained within a capitalist framework by maintaining and extending a development model focused on exports, exploitation of natural resources and a policy of low wages in order to remain competitive – although admittedly they have practised a policy of subsidies which did reduce poverty in the early years. One positive point is that the constitutions of Venezuela (1999), Ecuador (2008) and Bolivia (2009) include the principle of revocability of all mandates of elected representatives.

On the question of central banks, private banks and the finance sector in general, one can only notice an extremely serious impoverishment of the programmes of organizations who claim to be radically socialist. In 2019, the Manifesto of the Labour Party under the leadership of Jeremy Corbyn, although radical as regards a number of issues such as re-nationalizations and cancellation of student debt, says nothing about the City of London and the Bank of England; Bernie Sanders's 2019-2020 platform, radical in the areas of taxes and student debt, was also silent as regards the central bank (the *Fed*) and the big private banks. The programmes of other political organizations such as Podemos, DiEM25,[10] and Die Linke are either silent or else take a moderate and therefore inappropriate attitude towards the question of the central bank, big private banks, currency and public debt.

Greece 2015 or the failure of the moderate approach

 Action should have been taken to deal with the banks as soon as the Tsipras government was put in place. With the European Central Bank taking the initiative to worsen Greece's banking crisis, action should have been taken as provided for in the Thessaloniki Programme, on the basis of which the Syriza government was elected on 25 January 2015 and which stated: "With Syriza in government, the public sector will take over control of the Hellenic Financial Stability Fund (HFSF) and exercise all its rights over the recapitalized banks. That means that it will make decisions about the way they are run."

Bear in mind that in 2015 the Greek State, via the HFSF, was the principal shareholder of the country's four largest banks, accounting for over 85% of Greece's entire banking sector. The problem is that despite the numerous successive recapitalizations of Greek banks since October 2008, the State had no real weight in the banks' decisions since the shares it held did not entitle it to voting rights, as no previous government had made the necessary political decision. That being the case, the Parliament, in conformity with Syriza's commitments, should have turned the so-called preferential shares (having no voting rights associated with them) held by the public authorities into common shares with voting rights. Then the State, in a perfectly normal and legal way, would have been able to exercise its responsibilities and provide a solution to the banking crisis.

Lastly, five other important measures needed to be taken:

1. To face the banking and financial crisis that had been exacerbated by the *Troika* (the European Commission, the ECB and the IMF) since December 2014, which warned of bank failures, and by the ECB's decision of 4 February 2015, the government should have implemented oversight over capital movements in order to end flight of capital abroad.

2. Payments of external public debt should have been suspended with immediate effect.

3. The Governor of Greece's Central Bank should have been replaced and it should have been taken over in the name of the people.

4. The government should have set up a complementary currency and prepared to exit the euro.

5. It should have cancelled all working-class debts to private banks and the State.

The decision made by Prime Minister Tsipras and Finance Minister Varoufakis not to touch the private banks, to leave the former Governor of the Greek Central Bank in office, not to control capital flows and not to suspend repayment of the debt had dire consequences for the Greek people. To paraphrase Friedrich Engels' words about the Paris Commune, Tsipras and Varoufakis showed a sacred respect towards finance, they stopped before the portals of the Central Bank and the private banks. A historic opportunity was missed. That must not happen elsewhere in the world.

Conclusion

A popular government cannot sit back and do nothing in face of the world of Finance. It must take radical measures regarding its Central Bank, private banks and debt. If it does not do so, it is condemned to failure.

Notes

1. To satisfy the demands of the bourgeoisie, Thiers's government of and the Assembly dominated by conservative sectors favourable to the Prussian occupation had decided at the beginning of 1871 to end the moratorium on private debts, negotiable instruments and rents that crushed and squeezed the destitute Parisian population.

2. Here you will find the decrees concerning rents and pawn-shops in French only:https://macommunedeparis.com/2016/05/17/non-la-commune-na-pas-16-premiers-decrets/.

3. Pawn-brokers, or *Monts-de-piété* in French, were private institutions with share-holders who made a lot of profit. In 1869, they made 784 736, 53 francs. The annual turn-over was 25 million francs. There were about 40 branches in Paris. How it functioned: you handed over your item, known as a pawn or pledge, in exchange for a loan of 3 or 4 francs. You could redeem your pawn by paying interest of 12 to 15 per cent. If you did not redeem it within the agreed time, your item would simply be sold to the highest bidder. (English version adapted from: "The Commune et le Mont-de-piete" (The Commune and Pawn-brokers), https://macommunedeparis.com/2016/05/17/la-commune-et-le-mont-de-piete/) In a way, pawn-brokers foreshadow the private microcredit organizations that have appeared in developing countries over the last quarter of the 20th century.

4. See the book by Jean Baptiste Clément, *La Revanche des communeux*, Paris, 1887. It is a mine of information, particularly

on the situation of the working classes and on the debates that took place in The Commune accessible online in French, https://fr.wikisource.org/wiki/La_Revanche_des_communeux/Texte_entier.

5. For a more complete list of social measures see the 1891 Introduction by Frederick Engels to Marx's book, *The Civil War in France*, (1871), [Historical Background and Overview of the Civil War]. https://www.marxists.org/archive/marx/works/1871/civil-war-france. See Appendix 1 of this article.

6. Maxime Du Camp, *La Banque de France pendant la commune,* "III. Les dernières réquisitions, l'ensablement des caves". *Revue des Deux Mondes*, 3e période, tome 27, 1878 (p. 831-865).

7. See "The Programme of the Parti Ouvrier" https://www.marxists.org/archive/marx/works/1880/05/parti-ouvrier.htm.

8. Eric Toussaint, "Russia: Origin and consequences of the debt repudiation of February 10, 1918", https://www.cadtm.org/Russia-Origin-and-consequences-of-the-debt-repudiation-of-February-10-1918.

9. See Eric Toussaint, Fernando Martinez Heredia, *Du 19e au 21e siècle : une mise en perspective historique de la Révolution cubaine* (From the 19th to the 21st centuries: A historical perspective of the Cuban revolution) https://www.cadtm.org/Du-19e-au-21e-siecle-une-mise-en (in French or Spanish).

10. See Eva Betavatzi, Éric Toussaint and Olivier Bonfond, *The DiEM25 Plan to Confront the Covid-19 Crisis in Europe*, 26 May 2020, https://www.cadtm.org/The-DiEM25-Plan-to-Confront-the-Covid-19-Crisis-in-Europe.

Appendix 1

Frederick Engels's summary of the various measures taken by the Commune

. . . Thiers, the new head of government, was compelled to realize that the supremacy of the propertied classes – large landowners and capitalists – was in constant danger so long as the workers of Paris had arms in their hands. His first action was to attempt to disarm them. On 18 March, he sent troops of the line with orders to rob the National Guard of the artillery belonging to it, which had been constructed during the siege of Paris and had been paid for by public subscription. The attempt failed; Paris mobilized as one man in defence of the guns, and war between Paris and the French government sitting at Versailles was declared. On 26 March the Paris Commune was elected and on 28 March it was proclaimed. The Central Committee of the National Guard, which up to then had carried on the government, handed in its resignation to the National Guard, after it had first decreed the abolition of the scandalous Paris "Morality Police." On 30 March the Commune abolished conscription and the standing army, and declared that the National Guard, in which all citizens capable of bearing arms were to be enrolled, was to be the sole armed force. It remitted all payments of rent for dwelling houses from October 1870 until April, the amounts already paid to be reckoned to a future rental period, and stopped all sales of articles pledged in the municipal pawnshops. On the same day the foreigners elected to the Commune were confirmed in office, because "the flag of the Commune is the flag of the World Republic."

On 1 April it was decided that the highest salary received by any employee of the Commune, and therefore also by its members themselves, might not exceed 6,000 francs. On the following day the Commune decreed the separation of the Church from the State, and the abolition of all state payments for religious purposes as well as the transformation of all Church property into national property; as a result of which, on 8 April, a decree excluding from the schools all religious symbols, pictures, dogmas, prayers – in a word, "all that belongs to the sphere of the individual's conscience" – was ordered to be excluded from the schools, and this decree was gradually applied. On 5 April, in reply to the shooting, day after day, of the Commune's fighters captured by the Versailles troops, a decree was issued for imprisonment of hostages, but it was never carried into effect. On 6 April, the guillotine was brought out by the 137th battalion of the National Guard, and publicly burnt, amid great popular rejoicing. On the 12th, the Commune decided that the Victory Column on the Place Vendôme, which had been cast from guns captured by Napoleon after the war of 1809, should be demolished as a symbol of chauvinism and incitement to national hatred. This decree was carried out on 16 May. On 16 April the Commune ordered a statistical tabulation of factories which had been closed down by the manufacturers, and the working out of plans for the carrying on of these factories by workers formerly employed in them, who were to be organized in co-operative societies, and also plans for the organization of these co-operatives in one great union. On 20 April the Commune abolished night work for bakers, and also the workers' registration cards, which since the Second Empire had been run as a monopoly by police nominees – exploiters of the first rank; the issuing of these registration cards was transferred to the mayors of the 20 arrondissements of Paris. On 30 April, the Commune ordered the closing of the pawnshops, on the ground that they were a private exploitation of labour, and were in contradiction with the right of the workers to their instruments of labour and to credit. On 5 May it ordered the demolition of the Chapel of Atonement, which had been built in expiation of the execution of Louis XVI.

Appendix 2

Prosper-Olivier Lissagaray on the Commune and the Bank of France

In allowing the Versaillese army to march off, the Central Committee had committed a heavy fault; that of the Council was incomparably more damaging. All serious rebels have commenced by seizing upon the sinews of the enemy - the treasury. The Council of the Commune was the only revolutionary Government that refused to do so. While abolishing the budget of public worship, which was at Versailles, they bent their knees to the budget of the bourgeoisie, which was at their mercy.

Then followed a scene of high comedy, if one could laugh at negligence that has caused so much bloodshed. Since the 19 March the governors of the bank lived like men condemned to death, every day expecting the execution of the treasure. Of removing it to Versailles they could not dream. It would have required sixty or eighty vans and an army corps. On 23 March, its governor, Rouland, could no longer stand it, and fled. The deputy governor, De Ploeuc, replaced him. From his first interview with the delegates of the Hôtel-de-Ville he had seen through their timidity, given battle, then seemed to soften, yielded little by little, and doled out his money franc by franc. The bank, which Versailles believed almost empty, contained: coin, 77 million;[1] bank-notes, 166 million; bills discounted, 899 million; securities for advances made, 120 million; bullion, 11 million; jewels in deposit, 7 million; public effects and other titles in deposit, 900 million; that is, 2 milliards 180 million francs: 800 million in bank-notes only required the signature of the cashier, a signature easily made. The Commune had then three billion in its hands, of which over a billion was realized, enough to buy all the generals and func-tionaries of Versailles; as hostages, 90,000 depositors of titles, and the two billion in circulation whose guarantee lay in the coffers in the Rue de la Vrillière.

On 29 March old Beslay presented himself before the tabernacle. De Ploeuc had mustered his 430 clerks, armed with muskets without cartridges. Beslay, led through the lines of these warriors, humbly prayed the governor to be so kind as to supply the pay of the Na-tional Guard. De Ploeuc answered superciliously, spoke of defend-ing himself. 'But,' said Beslay, 'if, to prevent the effusion of blood, the Commune appointed a governor... "A governor! Never!' said De Ploeuc, who understood his man; 'but a delegate! If you were that delegate we might come to an understanding.' And, acting pathetic, 'Come, M. Beslay, help me to save this. This is the fortune of your country; this is the fortune of France.'

Beslay, deeply moved, hurried off to the Executive Commission, repeated his lesson all the better that he believed it and prided him-self on his financial lore. 'The bank,' he said, 'is the fortune of the country: without it, no more industry, no more commerce. If you violate it, all its notes will be so much waste-paper.[2] This trash cir-culated in the Hôtel-de-Ville, and the Proudhonists of the Council, forgetting that their master put the suppression of the bank at the head of his revolutionary programme, backed old Beslay. At Ver-sailles itself, the capitalist stronghold had no more inveterate de-fenders than those of the Hôtel-de-Ville. If someone had at least proposed, 'Let us at least occupy the bank' - but the Executive Com-mission had not the nerve to do this, and contented itself with commissioning Beslay. De Ploeuc received the good man with open arms, installed him in the nearest office, even persuading him to sleep at the bank, made him his hostage, and once more breathed freely.

Thus from the first week the Assembly of the Hôtel-de-Ville showed itself weak towards the authors of the sortie, weak towards the Central Committee, weak towards the bank, trifling in its decrees, in the choice of its delegate to the War Office, without a military plan, without a programme, without general views, and indulging in desultory discussions. The Radicals who had remained in the Council saw whither it was drifting, and, not inclined to play the martyrs, they sent in their resignations.

Notes

1. Mr Beslay, in his book *Mes Souvenirs,* Paris, 1873, says: "The cash in hand was forty and some odd millions." These "some odd" were no less than 203 millions. They presented the good man fictitious statements, with which they gulled him. In his evidence and the annexes (*Enquête sur le 18 Mars*, Vol. III, errata, p. 438), Mr de Ploeuc has given the true statements.

2. These were all the reasons he could ever allege, even in his book written in Switzerland, whither M. de Ploeuc himself went to deposit him after the fall of the Commune. Besides his life being saved, he, later on, received a judicial ordinance to the effect that no further judicial proceedings were to be taken against him.

11

Sources

The Paris Commune of 1871 by Michael Löwy, was translated by *International Viewpoint* and published on 18 March 2021, https://internationalviewpoint.org/spip.php?article7075.

Remembering the Paris Commune, Kay Mann. First published in *Against the Current,* No. 153, July/August 2011, https://againstthecurrent.org/atc153/p3315/#N4.

In Memory of the Commune, V.I. Lenin. First published in *Rabochaya Gazeta*, No. 4–5, 15 (28) April 1911; *Marxist Internet Archive,* https://www.marxists.org/archive/lenin/works/1911/apr/15.htm.

Do you know Lefrançais?, Daniel Bensaïd. This text is the preface to *Souvenirs d'un révolutionnaire. De juin 1848 à la Commune,* Paris: La Fabrique, 2013. It was translated by International Viewpoint, http://danielbensaid.org/Connaissez-vous-Lefrancais.

All the more monstrous because they were women. Interview of Mathilde Larrère conducted by Yohann Emmanuel for *l'Anticapitaliste la revue*, No.122, January 2021.

Genderquake: socialist women and the Paris Commune, Judy Cox. First published in *International Socialism*, No. 169, 5 January 2021, http://isj.org.uk/genderquake-paris-commune/.

The Commune is an ode to emancipation, which crosses time. Interview of Olivier Besancenot conducted by Julien Salingue. Published in the *Hebdo l'Anticapitaliste*, No. 560, 18 March 2021.

The Paris Commune of 1871, banks and debt, Eric Toussaint. First published by *the Committee for the Abolition of Illegitimate Debt*, 18 March 2021, https://www.cadtm.org/The-Paris-Commune-of-1871-banks-and-debt.

Frederick Engels's summary of the various measures taken by the Commune (Appendix 1, Chapter 10). First published in Frederick Engels' *Introduction to Marx, The Civil War in France (1871)*, *Marxist Internet Archive*, https://www.marxists.org/archive/marx/works/1871/civil-war-france/intro.htm.

Prosper-Olivier Lissagaray on the Commune and the Bank of France (Appendix 2, Chapter 10). First published in Prosper-Olivier Lissagaray's *History of the Paris Commune of 1871*, translated by Eleanor Marx, Chapter XIV, "The weaknesses of the Council", *Marxist Internet Archive*, https://www.marxists.org/history/france/archive/lissagaray/.

Events is based on the "Timeline of The Civil War in France", published by the *Marxist Internet Archive*, https://www.marxists.org/history/france/paris-commune/timeline.htm.

12

Events

A Timeline of The Civil War in France

1870

10 January: About 100,000 people demonstrate against Bonaparte's Second Empire after the death of Victor Noir, a republican journalist killed by the Emperor's cousin, Pierre Bonaparte.

8 May: A national plebiscite votes confidence in the Empire with about 84 per cent of votes in favour. On the eve of the plebiscite members of the Paris Federation of the International Workingmen's Association were arrested on a charge of conspiring against Napoleon III. This pretext was further used by the government to launch a campaign of persecution of the members of the International throughout France.

19 July: After a diplomatic struggle over the Prussian attempt for the Spanish throne, Louis Bonaparte declares war on Prussia.

23 July: Marx completes what will become known as his "First Address."

26 July: The "First Address" is approved and internationally distributed by the General Council of the International Workingmen's Association.

4-6 August: Crown Prince Frederick, commanding one of the three Prussian armies invading France, defeats French Marshal MacMahon at Worth and Weissenburg, pushes him out of Alsace (northeastern France), surrounds Strasbourg, and drives on towards Nancy. The other two Prussian armies isolate Marshal Bazaine's forces in Metz.

16-18 August: French Commander Bazaine's efforts to break his soldiers through the German lines are bloodily defeated at Mars-la-Tour and Gravelotte. The Prussians advance on Chalons.

1 September: Battle of Sedan. MacMahon and Bonaparte, attempting to relieve Bazaine at Metz and finding the road closed, enters battle and is defeated at Sedan.

2 September: Emperor Napoleon III and Marshal MacMahon capitulate at Sedan with over 83,000 soldiers.

4 September: In response to the news of Sedan, Parisian workers invade the Palais Bourbon and force the Legislative Assembly to proclaim the fall of the Empire. By evening, the Third Republic is proclaimed at the Hotel de Ville (the City Hall) in Paris. The provisional Government of National Defence (GND) is established to continue the war effort to remove Germany from France.

5 September: A series of meetings and demonstrations begin in London and other big cities, at which resolutions and petitions were passed demanding that the British Government immediately recognize the French Republic. The General Council of the First International took a direct part in the organization of this movement.

6 September: GND issues statement: blames war on Imperial government, it now wants peace, but "not an inch of our soil, not a stone of our fortresses, will we cede." With Prussia occupying Alsace-Lorraine, the war does not stop.

19 September: Two German armies begin the long siege of Paris. Bismarck figures the "soft and decadent" French workers will quickly surrender. The GND sends a delegation to Tours, soon to be joined by Gambetta (who escapes from Paris in a balloon), to organize resistance in the provinces.

27 October: French army, led by Bazaine with 140,000-180,000 men at Metz, surrenders.

30 October: French National Guard defeated at Le Bourget.

31 October: Upon the receipt of news that the Government of National Defence had decided to start negotiations with the Prussians, Paris workers and revolutionary sections of the National Guard rise up in revolt, led by Blanqui. They seize the *Hôtel de Ville* (City Hall) and set up their revolutionary government - the Committee of Public Safety, headed by Blanqui. On October 31, Flourens prevents any members of the Government of National Defence from being shot, as had been demanded by one of the insurrectionists.

1 November: Under pressure from the workers the Government of National Defence promises to resign and schedule national elections to the Commune - promises it has no intention to deliver. With the workers pacified by their 'legal' charade, the government violently seizes the *Hôtel de Ville* and re-establishes its domination over the besieged city. Paris official Blanqui is arrested for treason.

1871

22 January: The Paris proletariat and the National Guards hold a revolutionary demonstration, initiated by the Blanquists. They demand the overthrow of the government and the establishment of a Commune. By order of the Government of National Defence, the Breton Mobile Guard, which was defending the *Hôtel de Ville*, opens fire on the demonstrators. After massacring the unarmed workers, the government begins preparations to surrender Paris to the Germans.

28 January: After four long months of workers struggle, Paris is surrendered to the Prussians. While all regular troops are disarmed, the National Guard is permitted to keep their arms — the populous of Paris remains armed and allows the occupying armies only a small section of the city.

8 February: Elections held in France, unknown to most of the nation's population.

12 February: New National Assembly opens at Bordeaux; two-thirds of members are conservatives and wish the war to end.

16 February: The Assembly elects Adolphe Thiers Chief Executive.

26 February: The preliminary peace treaty between France and Germany signed at Versailles by Thiers and Jules Favre, on the one hand, and Bismarck, on the other. France surrenders Alsace and East Lorraine to Germany and promised to pay it indemnities to the sum of 5 billion francs. The final peace treaty was signed in Frankfort-on-Main on 10 May 1871.

1-3 March: After months of struggle and suffering, Paris workers react angrily to the entry of German troops in the city, and the ceaseless capitulation of the government. The National Guard defects and organizes a Central Committee.

10 March: The National Assembly passes a law on the deferred payment of overdue bills; under this law the payment of debts on obligations concluded between 13 August and 12 November 1870 could be deferred. Thus, the law leads to the bankruptcy of many petty bourgeoisie.

11 March: National Assembly adjourns. With trouble in Paris, it establishes its government at Versailles on 20 March.

18 March: Adolphe Thiers attempts to disarm Paris and sends French troops (regular army), but, through fraternization with Paris workers, they refuse to carry out their orders. Generals Claude Martin Lecomte and Jacques Leonard Clement Thomas are killed by their own soldiers. Many troops peacefully withdraw, some remain in Paris. Thiers is outraged, the Civil War begins.

26 March: A municipal council - the Paris Commune - is elected by the citizens of Paris. Commune consists of workers, among them members of the First International and followers of Proudhon and Blanqui.

28 March: The Central Committee of the National Guard, which up to then had carried on the government, resigns after it first decrees the permanent abolition of the "Morality Police".

30 March: The Commune abolishes conscription and the standing army; the National Guard, in which all citizens capable of bearing arms were to be enrolled, was to be the sole armed force. The Commune remits all payments of rent for dwelling houses from October 1870 until April 1871. On the same day the foreigners elected to the Commune were confirmed in office, because "the flag of the Commune is the flag of the World Republic".

1 April: The Commune declares that the highest salary received by any member of the Commune does not exceed 6,000 francs

2 April: In order to suppress the Paris Commune Thiers appeals to Bismarck for permission to supplement the Versailles Army with French prisoners of war, most of whom had been serving in the armies that surrendered at Sedan and Metz. In return for the 5 billion francs indemnity payment, Bismarck agrees. The French Army begins siege of Paris. Paris is continually bombarded and, moreover, by the very people who had stigmatized as a sacrilege the bombardment of the same city by the Prussians. The Commune decrees the separation of the Church from the State, and the abolition of all state payments for religious purposes as well as the transformation of all Church property into national property. Religion is declared a purely private matter.

5 April: Decree on hostages adopted by the Commune in an attempt to prevent Communards from being shot by the French Government. Under this decree, all persons found guilty of being in contact with the French Government were declared hostages. This was never carried out.

6 April: The guillotine was brought out by the 137th battalion of the National Guard, and publicly burnt, amid great popular rejoicing.

7 April: The French army captures the Seine crossing at Neuilly, on the western front of Paris. Reacting to French government policy of shooting captured Communards, Commune issues an "eye-for-an-eye" policy statement, threatening retaliation. The bluff is quickly called; Paris workers execute no one.

8 April: A decree excluding from the schools all religious symbols, pictures, dogmas, prayers - in a word, "all that belongs to the sphere of the individual's conscience" - is ordered to be excluded from the schools. The decree is gradually applied.

11 April: In an attack on southern Paris the French army is repulsed with heavy losses by General Eudes.

12 April: The Commune decides that the Victory Column on the Place Vendôme, which had been cast from guns captured by Napoleon after the war of 1809, should be demolished as a symbol of chauvinism and incitement to national hatred. This decree was carried out on 16 May.

16 April: Commune announces the postponement of all debt obligations for three years and abolition of interest on them. The Commune orders a statistical tabulation of factories which had been closed down by the manufacturers, and the working out of plans for the carrying on of these factories by workers formerly employed in them, who were to be organized in co-operative societies, and also plans for the organization of these co-operatives in one great union.

20 April: The Commune abolishes night work for bakers, and also the workers' registration cards, which since the Second Empire had been run as a monopoly by police nominees - exploiters of the first rank; the issuing of these registration cards was transferred to the mayors of the 20 *arrondissements* of Paris.

23 April: Thiers breaks off the negotiations for the exchange, proposed by Commune, of the Archbishop of Paris [Georges Darboy] and a whole number of other priests held hostages in Paris, for only one man, Blanqui, who had twice been elected to the Commune but was a prisoner in Clairvaux.

27 April: In sight of the impending municipal elections of 30 April, Thiers enacted one of his great conciliation scenes. He exclaimed from the tribune of the Assembly: "There exists no conspiracy against the republic but that of Paris, which compels us to shed French blood. I repeat it again and again...". Out of 700,000 municipal councillors, the united Legitimists, Orleanists, and Bonapartists (Party of Order) did not carry 8,000.

30 April: The Commune orders the closing of the pawnshops, on the ground that they were a private exploitation of labour and were in contradiction with the right of the workers to their instruments of labour and to credit.

5 May: The Commune ordered the demolition of the Chapel of Atonement, which had been built in expiation of the execution of Louis XVI.

9 May: Fort Issy, which is completely reduced to ruins by gunfire and constant French bombardment, is captured by the French army.

10 May: The peace treaty concluded in February now signed, known as Treaty of Frankfurt. (Endorsed by National Assembly 18 May.)

16 May: The Vendôme Column is pulled down. The Vendôme Column was erected between 1806 and 1810 in Paris in honour of the victories of Napoleonic France; it was made out of the bronze captured from enemy guns and was crowned by a statue of Napoleon.

21-28 May: Versailles troops enter Paris on 21 May. The Prussians who held the northern and eastern forts allowed the Versailles troops to advance across the land north of the city, which was forbidden ground to them under the armistice - Paris workers held the flank with only weak forces. As a result of this, only a weak resistance was put up in the western half of Paris, in the luxury city; while it grew stronger and more tenacious the nearer the Versailles troops approached the eastern half, the working class city.

The French army spent eight days massacring workers, shooting civilians on sight. The operation was led by Marshal MacMahon, who would later become president of France. Tens of thousands of Communards and workers are summarily executed (as many as 30,000); 38,000 others imprisoned and 7,000 are forcibly deported.

13

People

Arnould, Arthur (17 April 1833 – 26 November 1895). Libertarian writer and journalist. Participated actively in the Commune and the First International.

Auclert, Marie Anne Hubertine (10 April 1848 – 8 April 1914). Journalist, writer and feminist activist, fought for the right to vote.

Beslay, Charles Victor (1795 – 1878). The oldest member of the Paris Commune. He considered his role was to protect the Bank of France against the "extreme" elements of the Commune.

Blanqui, Louis Auguste (8 February 1805 – 1 January 1881). Socialist activist from the 1830s. Arrested on 17 March he was elected president of the insurgent Commune. The Communards offered to release all of their prisoners if the Thiers government released Blanqui, but this was refused and he was thus prevented from taking an active part. He was nevertheless judged and condemned to life imprisonment in November 1871 (escaping deportation because of his age and health) and eventually released in 1879.

Brocher, **Victorin**e (4 September 1839 – 4 November 1921). Communard, anarchist writer and speaker. Wrote her memoirs *Souvenir d'une morte vivante*, about her participation in the Commune. After the Commune lived in Switzerland, Hungary, London as well as returning to France. Died in Lausanne.

Carnot, **Count Lazare Nicolas Marguerite** (13 May 1753 – 2 August 1823). Leading figure of the French revolutionary government.

Clément, **Jean Baptiste** (31 May 1836 – 23 February 1903). Member of the Commune and author of the songs *Le Temps des Cerises* and *La Semaine sanglante* closely associated with it.

Courbet, **Jean Désiré Gustave** (10 June 1819 – 31 December 1877). Active member of the Commune, a painter who led the Realism movement in 19th-century French painting.

De Plœuc, **Alexandre** (7 October 1815 – 25 August 1887. French noble and director of the Bank de France during the Commune.

De Rothschild, **Alphonse** (1 February 1827 – 26 May 1905), French banker.

Deraismes, **Marie Adélaïde**, known as Maria (17 August 1828 – 6 February 1894). Feminist, speaker and writer who worked with Louise Michel, Paule Minck and others on women's rights.

Deroin, **Jeanne** (31 December 1805 – 2 April 1894). Socialist feminist active in the 1848 revolutions. Lived in exile in London from 1852, where she continued to be politically active.

Dmitrieff (Dimitrieff) Elisabeth (born Elizabeta Luknichna Kusheleva (Tomanovskaya), 1 November 1850, Russia – 1910 or

1918 Russia). Feminist and revolutionary, a co-founder of the Women's Union in the Paris Commune. Member of the First International.

Dombrowski, Jaroslaw (13 April (or 12 November) 1836 – 23 May 1871). Polish soldier, condemned to forced labour in Siberia for insurrectional activities in Poland, escaped and made his way to Paris. Member of the First International. Named general of the Commune, mortally wounded on the barricades.

Dreyfus, Alfred (9 October 1859 – 12 July 1935). Army captain of Jewish origin who was accused of handing secrets to the Germans. This created a political scandal known as the Dreyfus Affair (1894-1906). It strongly divided public opinion with strong accusations of antisemitism. Dreyfus was finally exonerated and reinstated in the army.

Durand, Marguerite (24 January 1864 – 16 March 1936). Actress, journalist, and leading suffragette.

Du Camp, Maxime (8 February 1822 – 8 February 1894). French writer and photographer, member of the *Académie française*. Wrote a hostile history of the Commune *Les convulsions de Paris*.

Excoffon, Béatrix, (born Julia Euvrie ou Œuvrie 10 July 1849 – 30 December 1916). Republican activist, and an ambulance nurse during the Commune. She was known as "La Républicaine".

Flourens, Gustave (4 August 1838 in Paris – 3 April 1871). One of the most active leaders of the insurrection, was captured, disarmed and killed on 3 April.

Franckel, Leo (25 February 1844, Újlak– 29 March 1896, Paris). Leading member of the Commune of Hungarian and Jewish origin.

Gambetta, Léon (2 April 1838 – 31 December 1882). Lawyer and politician. A republican he was opposed to the Commune.

Guesde, Jules (11 November 1845 – 28 July 1922) (born Jules Bazile). Socialist journalist and politician. He was the inspiration for a famous quotation by Karl Marx: "what is certain is that [if he is], [then] I myself am not a Marxist".

Hugo, Victor (7 Ventôse year X [26 February 1802] – 22 May 1885). Writer who evolved from conservative positions in 1848 to more radical, if ambiguous, ones by the time of the Commune.

Jaclard, Anna (born Anna Vassilievna Korvin-Krukovsky 18 October 1843 – 14 September 1887). Russian socialist feminist and revolutionary. Active in the Commune and member of the First International. Friend of Karl Marx and Fyodor Dostoeyevsky.

Jaclard, Victor (18 December 1840 – 14 April 1903). One of the first French socialists, member of the First International and leader of the Commune.

Kawecka, Lodoyska, of Polish origin, active in the women's clubs and in the armed defence of the Commune.

Lafargue, Paul (15 January 1842 – 25 November 1911). Active member of the First International, married Laura Marx in 1868 while in exile in London. In France during the Commune then fled to Spain, and then to London. Returned to France in 1882, was elected as a socialist to parliament in 1891. Died in a suicide pact with Laura.

Lefrançais, Gustave Adolphe (30 January 1826 – 16 May 1901). Revolutionary anarchist, member of First International, and president of the Paris Commune,

Lemel, Nathalie (26 August 1827 – 1921). Militant anarchist and feminist and leading activist and fighter of the Commune. She was deported to Nouvelle Calédonie with Louise Michel.

Léo, André (born Victoire Léodile Béra, 18 August 1824 – 20 May 1900). Novelist, journalist and early feminist activist. She played a leading role in the Commune.

Lefebvre, Blanche (1847 – 23 May 1871). Laundress, member of the Social Revolution Club and Women's Union, killed on the barricades in Bloody Week.

Lissagaray, Prosper Olivier "Lissa" (24 November 1838 – 25 January 1901). Journalist was a strong defender of the Commune although not holding any formal role. In exile afterwards he lived with the Marx family and became engaged to Eleanor who translated his *History of the Paris Commune of 1871*.

Longuet, Charles Félix César (14 February 1839 – 5 August 1903). In exile in London after the Commune married Jenny Marx.

Malon, Benoît (23 June 1841 – 13 September 1893). Journalist and writer, one of the founders of the First International, elected member of the Paris Commune.

Marx, Jenny (Longuet) (1 May 1844 – 11 January 1883). Second daughter of Karl Marx. Married Charles Longuet while he was in exile after the Commune. Followed him to France in 1881 but died in 1882 two months before her father.

Michel, Louise (29 May 1830 – 9 January 1905). Probably the best-known woman of the Commune, and was a teacher. Was transported to New Caledonia and on return to France emerged as an important French anarchist and went on speaking tours across Europe. Her use of a black flag at a demonstration in Paris in March 1883 is also the earliest known use of the anarchist black flag.

Michelet, Jules (21 August 1798 – 9 February 1874). Anti-clericalist and republican wrote a major History of the French Revolution.

Mink (Minck), Paule (9 November 1839 – 28 April 1901) was of Polish origins (born Adèle Pauline Mekarski). A socialist and feminist journalist she participated actively in the creation of women's clubs during the Commune. Absent from Paris at the defeat of Commune she stayed in exile in Switzerland until the 1880 amnesty.

Noir, Victor (27 July 1848 – 11 January 1870). Journalist. After he was shot and killed by Prince Pierre Bonaparte a cousin of the Emperor Napoleon III he became a symbol of opposition to the imperial regime.

Pottier, Eugène Edine (4 October 1816 – 6 November 1887). Elected member of the Commune, poet and songwriter, author of The Internationale. Took refuge near London after the defeat of the Commune. From 1874 to 1880 he was in the USA, he then returned to France.

Proudhon, Pierre-Joseph (15 January 1809 – 19 January 1865). Described himself as an anarchist and socialist, influential in the French socialist movement. His best known assertion is "Property is theft". However, he is and was particularly known and criticized for his misogynistic positions: a woman's choice was to be "courtesan or housekeeper", to a woman, a man is "a father, a chief, a master: above all, a master".

Reclus, Élie (Jean-Pierre, Michel) (16 June 1827 – 11 February 1904). Director of the *Bibliothèque nationale* (National Library) under the Commune. He was a freemason..

Reclus, Noémi (23 March 1828 – 14 July 1905). Schoolteacher, feminist, Communard. After the Commune lived in Switzerland with her husband (and cousin) Elie Reclus.

Rigault, Raoul (16 September 1846 – 24 May 1871). Student, journalist, delegate to the *Sûreté générale* and prosecutor of the Commune. Shot dead near the Panthéon during the fighting.

Rouland, Gustave (3 February 1806 – 12 December 1878). Lawyer and politician. He was Governor of the Bank of France during the Commune.

Roland, Pauline (1805 – 15 December 1852). Feminist and socialist activist. One of the founders of the Socialist Teachers' Association, wrote histories of France, England, Scotland and Ireland for children.

Saint-Simon, Henri de (7 October 1760 – 19 May 1825). Political and economic theorist, precursor of socialism.

Schmitt, Marie (born 1837). Attached to the 101st Battalion with her husband Charles Léon Gaspard to manage the canteen. Fought during Bloody Week, she was arrested and deported to New Caledonia.

Thiers, Adolphe (15 April 1797 (26 Germinal An V) – 3 September 1877). Leading politician from 1830. Elected chief executive of the government in February 1871 he negotiated an armistice with the Prussians. Responsible for the fierce repression of the Commune.

Tinayre, Marguerite, Victoire, née Guerrier (6 March 1831 – 16 August 1895). Writer and schoolteacher she was a school inspector during the Commune. After the defeat she spent her years of exile in Switzerland and Hungary, before returning to France in 1880.

Tristan, Flora (7 April 1803 - 14 November 1844). Daughter of a Peruvian nobleman, grandmother of the painter Gauguin. Travelled extensively in France, England and to Peru writing about the lives of working people, advocated the need for a universal union of working men and women.

Vaillant, Édouard (26 January 1840 – 18 December 1915). Called for the creation of the Commune and was elected member where he had special responsibility for education. Member of the First International he was in exile from the Commune until the amnesty of 1880.

Vallès, Jules (11 June 1832 – 14 February 1885). Journalist and author. A leading and early member of the Commune he fought to the end and escaped to London via Belgium. He returned after the 1880 amnesty.

Varlin, Eugène (5 October 1839 – 28 May 1871). Socialist, communard and member of the First International. He was one of the pioneers of French syndicalism.

Vermorel, Auguste-Jean-Marie (21 June 1841 – 20 June 1871). Wounded on the barricades, died as a prisoner at Versailles.

Vincent, Eliska (née Girard 29 June 1841–19 February 1914). Early feminist activist, notably for the right to education. She was a supporter of the Commune.

Wolff, Marie (born 1849, married name Guyard). An ambulance nurse she also fought on the barricades. Condemned to death after the Commune she was then deported to French Guiana.

14

Bibliography

Abidor, Mitchell, 2010, *Communards: The Story of the Commune of 1871 as Told By Those Who Fought For It,* Marxists Internet Archive Publications.

Beisson, Georges, *La Commune et la Banque de France,* Association of the friends of the Paris Commune de 1871 (in French). https://www.commune1871.org/la-commune-de-paris/histoire-de-la-commune/dossier-thematique/les-services-publics/569-la-commune-et-la-banque-de-france.

Benjamin, Walter, 1968, "Theses on the Philosophy of History" in *Illuminations, Essays and Reflections,* Schocken Books.

Bloodworth, Sandra, 2005, "Militant spirits: the rebel women of Broken Hill". https://sa.org.au/interventions/rebelwomen/militant.htm.

Bloodworth, Sandra, 2013, "Lenin vs 'Leninism'", *Marxist Left Review,* 5, Summer. https://marxistleftreview.org/articles/lenin-vs-leninism/.

Buzzfeed, 2021, "Stormings of History Ranked from Best to Worst", January. https://www.buzzfeed.com/tessred/stormings-of-history-ranked-from-best-to-worst-dogxsiwtv3?utm_source=dynamic&utm_campaign=bfsharefacebook&fbclid=IwAR0Bm0V61 HcfuBZsc6jth8J51i6z-enf8-N_WefnVp1pITFqvlRQoAa9_kI.

Cox, Judy, 2021, "Genderquake: socialist women and the Paris Commune", *International Socialism*, 169, 5 January. http://isj.org.uk/genderquake-paris-commune/.

Du Camp, Maxime, 2015, *La Banque de France sous la Commune*, FB Editions (Herausgeber).

Edwards, Stewart (ed.), 1973, *The Communards of Paris, 1871* (*Documents of Revolution* series, Heinz Lubasz, general editor), Thames and Hudson.

Eichner, Caroline J, 2004, *Surmounting the Barricades: Women in the Paris Commune,* Indiana University Press.

Eschelbacher, Andrew, 2009, "Environment of Memory: Paris and Post-Commune Angst", *Nineteenth Century Art World*, 8 (2), Autumn. https://www.19thc-artworldwide.org/autumn09/environment-of-memory.

Gluckstein, Donny, 2006, *The Paris Commune. A Revolution in Democracy,* Bookmarks.

Gluckstein, Donny, 2008, "Decyphering the Internationale: The Eugène Pottier Code", *International Socialism 120* (autumn), https://isj.org.uk/decyphering-the-internationale-the-eugene-pottier-code.

Gluckstein, Donny, 2011, *The Paris Commune*, Haymarket Books.

Godineau, Dominique, 1988, *Citoyennes Tricoteuses*, Alinea.

Gullickson, Gay L, 1996, *Unruly Women of Paris: Images of the Commune*, Cornell University Press.

Hazan, Eric, 2011, *The Invention of Paris. A History in Footsteps*, translator David Fernbach, Verso.

Holmes, Rachel, 2014, *Eleanor Marx: A Life*, Bloomsbury.

Horton, Richard, 2021, "The Paris Commune and the birth of American medicine", *The Lancet*, 397, (102070), 16 January. https://www.thelancet.com/journals/lancet/article/ PIIS0140-6736(21)00086-6/fulltext.

Jones, Kathleen, and Francois Verges, 1991, "'Aux citoyennes!': Women, Politics and the Paris Commune of 1871", *History of European Ideas*, volume 13, issue 6.

Jones, Kathleen, and Francois Verges, 1991, "Women of the Paris Commune", *Women's Studies International Forum*, volume 14, number 5.

Kouvelakis, Stathis, 2021 Introductory essay in *Sur la Commune de Paris textes de Karl Marx et Friedrich Engels,* Editions Sociales. English translation of Kouvelakis: https://www.versobooks.com/ blogs/5039-on-the-paris-commune-part-1.

Landrigan, Aloysius Judas, 2017, *Remembering the Commune: Texts and Celebrations in Britain and the United States,* MA thesis,

University of Melbourne. https://minerva-access.unimelb.edu.au/handle/11343/198112.

Lenin, Vladimir, 1917, "State and Revolution", in *Collected Works*, volume 25 (Progress), www.marxists.org/archive/lenin/works/1917/staterev.

Lenin, Vladimir, 1918, "Can the Bolsheviks Retain State Power?", in *Collected Works*, volume 26, www.marxists.org/archive/lenin/works/1917/oct/01.htm.

Lissagaray, Prosper Olivier, 1976 [1876], *History of the Paris Commune of 1871*, translator Eleanor Marx, New Park Publications and at https://www.marxists.org/history/france/archive/lissagaray/index.htm

Luxemburg, Rosa, 1919, "Order Prevails in Berlin", *Die Rote Fahne*, 14 January. https://www.marxists.org/archive/luxemburg/1919/01/14.htm

McClellan, Woodford, 1979, *Revolutionary Exiles: The Russians in the First International and the Paris Commune*, Routledge.

McMillan, James F, 2000, *France and Women 1789-1914: Gender, Society and Politics*, Routledge.

Mandel, Ernest, 1978, *De la Commune a mai 68 : histoire du mouvement ouvrier international*, Editions La Brèche (http://www.ernestmandel.org/new/ecrits/article/la-commune-n-est-pas-morte).

Marx, Karl, 1845, *Theses on Feuerbach*. https://www.marxists.org/archive/marx/works/1845/theses/theses.htm.

Marx, Karl, 1852, *The Eighteenth Brumaire of Louis Bonaparte.* https://www.marxists.org/archive/marx/works/1852/18th-bru-maire/.

Marx, Karl, 1871, *The Civil War in France* (includes First and Second Drafts*).* https://www.marxists.org/archive/marx/works/1871/civil-war-france/index.htm.

Marx-Engels *Collected Works,* Volume 23, Lawrence Wishart.

Marx, Karl and Friedrich Engels, 1932 [1846], *The German Ideology.* https://www.marxists.org/archive/marx/works/1845/german-ideology/index.htm.

Marx, Karl, Friedrich Engels, Mikhail Bakunin and Peter Kropotkin, 2008, *Writings on the Paris Commune*, Red and Black Publishers.

Merriman, John, 2016, *Massacre. The Life and Death of the Paris Commune of 1871*, Yale University Press.

Moon, Joan, 1978, "Feminism and Socialism: The Utopian Synthesis of Flora Tristan", in Marilyn J Boxer and Jean H Qutaert (eds), *Socialist Women: European Socialist Feminism in the Nineteenth and Early Twentieth Century,* Elsevier.

Ray, Claudine, 2012, "Louise et les autres, le combat des femmes dans la Commune", *Les Amies et Amis de la Commune de Paris 1871*, www.commune1871.org/la-commune-de-paris/histoire-de-la-commune/dossier-thematique/les-femmes-de-la-commune/564-louise-et-les-autres-le-combat-des-femmes-dans-la-commune.

Ross, Kristin, 2016, *Communal Luxury. The Political Imaginary of the Paris Commune*, Verso.

Schulkind, Eugene (ed), 1971, *The Paris Commune of 1871: The View from the Left*, Grove Press.

Schulkind, Eugene, 1985, "Socialist Women in the 1871 Paris Commune", *Past & Present*, volume 106, issue 1.

Singer-Lecocq, Yvonne, 2011, *Rouge Elisabeth*, Pascal Galodé.

Syson, Lydia, 2015, "Citoyennes: Women of the Paris Commune", Lydia Syson website, https://bit.ly/3pItK5r.

Thomas, Edith, 1966 [1963 as *Les Pétroleuses*], *The Women Incendiaries*, Secker and Warburg.

Tod, MK, 2020, *Poetry about the Paris Commune*, blog, 10 September. https://awriterofhistory.com/tag/poetry-about-the-paris-commune/.

RESISTANCE BOOKS publishes internationalist, ecosocialist, and feminist books. Resistance Books publishes books in collaboration with the International Institute for Research and Education (iire.org), and the Fourth International (https://fourth.international). For further information, including a full list of titles available and how to order them, go to the Resistance Books website.

info@resistancebooks.org – resistancebooks.org

THE INTERNATIONAL INSTITUTE FOR RESEARCH AND EDUCATION is a centre for the development of critical thought and the exchange of experiences and ideas. Since 1982, when the Institute opened in Amsterdam, it has organized courses for progressive forces around the world which deal with all subjects related to the emancipation of the oppressed and exploited. The IIRE provides activists and academics opportunities for research and education in three locations: Amsterdam, Islamabad and Manila.

iire@iire.org – iire.org

Lightning Source UK Ltd.
Milton Keynes UK
UKHW041556090521
383372UK00001B/97

9 780902 869431